UNLIMITED VALUE

-.-.-.-.-.-

Stories and Lessons from Yellowstone

Parks Collins and Bill Day

ISBN-13: 978-1983635144
ISBN-10: 1983635146

This resource is dedicated to Dr. Nelson Cooper, who passed away in May 2017 after living life well. Coop was part of *Project Yellowstone*'s early leadership team. He helped write grants and generated ideas for the structure of the program. He was most excited about spending time in God's creation. Coop was especially fond of our national parks. He loved teaching and sharing the experience with others. I'll always appreciate his willingness to listen to ideas and offer advice. Thanks, Coop.

UNLIMITED VALUE

Contents

PART IV … UNSOLICITED ADVICE

Preface

Project Yellowstone

–.–.–.–.–.–

IN 2002, AN OLD BOAR GRIZZLY MEANDERED ACROSS the road. Not just any grizzly. A wild grizzly. Not just any place. Yellowstone National Park.

Several years later, an idea hatched. Yellowstone could and should be used as an outdoor classroom for students. Students need a place where they can learn biological concepts by 1) seeing biology in action and 2) actually doing science. They need a place to learn experientially where phones don't work. Nature matters. The Greater Yellowstone Ecosystem (GYE) offers countless opportunities for learning and exploring biology. This diverse ecosystem, located in the northwest corner of Wyoming, has everything to explore from unique geology to predator/prey dynamics.

After conversations with intelligent people and generous financial support from the community, we were ready to offer a program to high school students. *Project Yellowstone* was created with a mission to make science relevant, allow students the opportunity to be scientists, and stimulate conservation through appreciation.

Nine students from Statesville High School (NC) participated in 2009. The students completed inquiry-based research projects, observed large megafauna such as bears, wolves, and moose, and hiked many of the trails. They explored the vegetation, the physical formations of the land, and the geothermal features. In 2010, nine more high school scholarship students participated in this program. The leadership team during those first two years included Chris Bowen, Danny Collins, and Dr. Nelson Cooper. They played a critical role in creating and establishing the structure of the program.

The program expanded in 2011 and 2012 to include students from Mitchell Community College (NC) in addition to the high school students. Adults from the community also participated during these years, which added an element of inter-generational learning. Tracy Snider, Harry Efird, Earl Spencer, John Ervin, Dr. John Karriker, and Dr. Nelson Cooper stepped up to serve as mentors to the students as they completed research projects in the park. Bill Day also came along in 2011 and has not missed a trip since. His vast knowledge and willingness to do whatever is needed coupled with his uncanny ability to spot wildlife is invaluable to the program.

Since 2014, we have offered the trip to anyone in the community. Having participants of all ages is vital to the success of this program.

In 1947, James Bryant Conant suggested that a scientist becomes a scientist when "curiosity about a phenomenon leads to an inquiry for new knowledge." He goes on to say that it doesn't matter whether the person has lots of accumulated knowledge about a particular subject. What makes a scientist a scientist is simply an "attitude of inquiry." This program seeks to engage participants and foster this attitude of inquiry.

In 1933, three authors wrote the following in the *Fauna of the National Parks of the United States*:

> "But our national heritage is richer than just scenic features; the realization is coming that perhaps our greatest national heritage is nature itself, with all its complexity and its abundance of life, which, when combined with great scenic beauty as it is in the national parks, becomes of unlimited value. This is what we would attain in the national parks."

This book is a collection of essays that shows some of the reasons why Yellowstone is special. We can learn a lot from this place. Nature has a story to tell. Nature holds a value that is unlimited. This book is based on notes and activities created for *Project Yellowstone*. Our hope is that others will find it helpful and informative.

Part One: Unusual Terrain

Nursery rock. This boulder was carried by a glacier. The rock created an ideal habitat for the Douglas fir, thus the name 'nursery' rock.

Chapter 1

Cold Times

−.−.−.−.−.−

While a glacier is moving, it rubs and wears down the bottom on which it moves, scrapes its surface (now smooth), triturates the broken-off material that is found between the ice and the rock, pulverizes or reduces it to a clayey paste, rounds angular blocks that resist its pressure, and polishes those having a larger surface.

- Louis Agassiz

FOLLOWING THE ROAD SOUTH FROM LIVINGSTON, Montana, you will soon find a classroom full of dangerous beasts, natural furnaces, and eerie sounds. Teaching science in the Greater Yellowstone Ecosystem (GYE) could have greater risks than teaching in a traditional classroom, but the potential rewards are significantly higher. Entering the area from the north, we are immediately hedged between two great mountain chains, the Gallatin range to the west and the Absaroka to the east. The Gallatin range extends more than seventy-five miles and is named for Albert Gallatin, the longest-serving U.S. Secretary of the Treasury under Presidents Jefferson and Madison. The Absaroka range stretches for 150 miles and eventually forms the eastern boundary of the park. Absaroka means "children of the large-beaked bird," and is named for the Absaroka, or Crow, Indians.

The Yellowstone River flows through this valley northward. It's the longest, un-dammed river in the country. Osprey nest close to the water, trout leap from the river and cottonwood trees line the banks with willows growing from the wetter areas. White-tailed deer stick to the cottonwoods, while the larger mule deer prefer to be in the sage. This part of the GYE becomes the perfect backdrop for a geology lesson.

The valley, called Paradise Valley, is mostly used for agricultural purposes today, but in its non-agricultural form, it is grassland and sagebrush. It gives us the perfect opportunity to talk about microclimates. There are more trees on the northern/eastern sides of the ridges than there are on the southern/western sides. The southern/western sides receive more direct sun than the northern/eastern sides, which dries the soil. Grasses and sagebrush tolerate dry conditions, so they dominate the southern and western sides of a slope. Thirsty trees tend to grow on northern and eastern sides. Geography determines where plants grow and thrive, and ultimately which animals tend to hang around. Oddly enough, the Yellowstone River played no role in carving this valley. Something larger and colder carved this valley.

The theory of continental glaciation came from Louis Agassiz. Agassiz, a scientist from Switzerland, knew quite a bit about mountain glaciers. His work in 1840 called "Etudes sur les glaciers" described the movements of glaciers. He hypothesized that the majority of North America had been covered in an ice sheet that was at least two miles thick and extended into the Midwest. Prior to this time, geologists did not even entertain the idea that glaciers could impact a landscape. They thought that it was flooding that moved dirt and rocks. After studying glaciers in Switzerland as well as in the western U.S., Agassiz came to believe that it was moving glaciers that carved the land.

The impact that glaciers have on land has been studied quite extensively since then. Glaciers currently makeup 10% of the world's total land area and are remnants of the last ice age. They form when more snow falls in the winter than melts in the summer. The fallen snow compresses into enormous ice masses when it stays in one location long enough, such as high on mountains. This is often seen in polar regions. Over time, the bottom layers melt due to the rise in temperature, and the top layers then slide due to gravity. Glaciers may range in size from a football field to hundreds of miles long. In fact, the most extensive glacier recorded is Lambert glacier in Antarctica, stretching 60 miles wide and 270 miles long. This huge ice sheet can do severe landscape demolition and redesign once it starts moving.

Paradise Valley was influential in the creation and development of the park's ecology because it was carved by glaciers from the Pinedale glacial period (70,000 years ago - 13,000 years ago). During this Pinedale period, glacial sheets extended from the poles to cover most of Canada, all of New England and much of the upper Midwestern U.S. Glaciers carved Paradise Valley and slowly deposited sediment and rock in the process. These glaciers were responsible for the rocks at the base of the Yellowstone River and also for the seemingly random boulders that are scattered about in the northern range of the park.

The Gallatin and Absaroka mountains with Paradise Valley between them were not the only places influenced by the glaciers from the Pinedale period. There's a much older range to the east that was impacted. The ecosystems of the Appalachian Mountains were changed by the flexing and contracting of glaciers. Glaciers can create valleys, but they can also distribute species, causing biodiversity to explode in some areas while limiting it in other areas. No other place shows this better than the Appalachian Mountains. The Appalachian range displays a great variety of biodiversity with the southern range being more diverse than the northern range. The Great Smokey Mountain National Park in the south has around 100 different native tree species and five major types of forests. How do you explain that? What limited biodiversity in the northern range, and what promoted it in the southern range?

The expansion of glaciers in the Appalachian Mountains caused major deforestation in the north thus limiting biodiversity. The flora that dominated the Canadian-zone gradually seeded southward and became established in the southern Appalachians. The northeast to southwest orientation of the Appalachian range made it easier for species to migrate southward along the slopes. This is how the southern Appalachians ended up with animal species such as the northern water shrew, the northern flying squirrel, and the spruce-fir moss spider. This process, animals and plants that are the same or closely related being geographically separated, is known as disjunct distribution.

Understanding the relationship between geologic processes and animal and plant distributions is not a recent field of study. One interesting story from the 1800s involves a leading botanist, the most celebrated biologist, and a small town in North Carolina.

Chapter 2

Searching for *Shortia*

- . - . - . -

As icebergs are known to be sometimes loaded with earth and stones, and have even carried brushwood, bones, and the nest of a land-bird, it can hardly be doubted that they must occasionally, as suggested by Lyell, have transported seeds from one part to another of the arctic and Antarctic regions; and during the Glacial period from one part of the now temperate regions to another.

- Charles Darwin

THE TRAIN CAME TO A SCREECHING HALT AT THE town depot, which sat atop a hill. The year was 1879. Asa Gray, a retired Harvard professor, gathered his belongings and gently stepped out of the car. Gray, who was once clean-shaven, had grown a large white beard. His hair, trimmed close to his head, was neatly combed and parted. He wore a black suit. As he stepped off, he appeared to be all business. On the inside, however, he could hardly contain his excitement. There was no media attention. Nor was there a gathering of people asking for an autograph, but there probably should have been.

Dr. Asa Gray was the nation's leading authority on plants and possibly America's greatest living scientist at the time. He had been searching for a plant for forty years, and it was this trip to Statesville, NC that he hoped would finally end the search. Statesville was going to bring relief to Gray, and in a sense, bring his career full-circle.

During Gray's tenure at Harvard, he had worked with and was overshadowed by Louis Agassiz. Agassiz had been hired in 1847 as a professor of zoology and geology soon after he first came to the U.S. to lecture in Boston. It did not matter to Gray that Agassiz commanded most of the attention at Cambridge and was friends with famous people like Ralph Waldo Emerson and Oliver Wendell Holmes. Gray was able to work on plants, the subject he loved best.

In 1838-39, Gray had traveled to Paris to network with other botanists and examine the original sources of American flora in several European herbaria. It was here in Paris where Gray began searching through the plant collections of noted scientist Andre Michaux (1746-1802). Michaux had spent eleven years in the U.S. collecting plants and sending them back to France. One plant caught Grey's attention. This specimen came with directions from Michaux so that other botanists might find it in the "High Mountains of Carolina."

What excited Gray was that this plant was probably a new genus that had yet to be studied or documented. He traveled several times (summers of 1841 and 1843) to the North Carolina mountain region to search for this plant with no luck. Gray did not realize it at the time, but the problem was that he was searching at elevations over 5,000 feet when this particular plant grows at a much lower altitude. At that time Gray was also busy working on a book about the flora of North America, so he did not have a lot of time to devote to this mystery plant. However, the plant, which Gray named *Shortia*, was never too far from his mind.

Mordecai Hyams, a local businessman and scientist, met Gray at the train station in Statesville. Hyams had been hired by the Confederacy during the Civil War to help process roots, herbs, and barks into medicinal drugs. These plant items were made into extracts, pills, powders, and ointments for the soldiers. After the war ended, Hyams went to work as a botanist and manager of the Wallace Brothers botanic depot, a three-story, 44,000 square foot warehouse in Statesville. Hyams' main responsibility was to organize expeditions in which he and others would gather and identify plants. It was during one of these expeditions that Hyams and his son, George, had collected *Shortia galacifolia*, Gray's mystery plant.

While in Statesville, Gray was also able to visit the Wallace Brothers herbarium warehouse. He wrote the following:

"A visit to the root and herb warehouse belonging to the Wallace brothers and under the charge of Mr. Hyams, furnished evidence that this branch of industry has reached an extent and importance of which few are aware. The printed catalogue of indigenous plants, dealt in by this house, enumerates about 630 species…These samples find a large market, both in this country and Europe, and the orders come mainly from the wholesale druggists and the manufacturers of patent medicines. Think of a single order for fifteen tons of *Hepatica triloba!*"

The Wallace brothers and Mordecai Hyams certainly had a great interest in plants because they were trying to make a profit by selling them for medicinal purposes. Gray, though, was not in the field of herbal remedies. So, why was this particular plant so important to Dr. Asa Gray? Why did he refer to it as "perhaps the most interesting plant in North America?"

At some point during the 1840s, Gray started exploring the idea of plant disjunction, the disjunct distribution of plants across the globe. He had noticed that eastern North America and eastern Asia both had plants that were found nowhere else in the world. More specifically, forty plant genera existed only in these two areas. Gray was intrigued by this relationship, but failed to study it carefully at the time. In 1855, Charles Darwin requested Gray's help in solving some plant-species distribution problems. Darwin wanted to know why plants and animals were distributed throughout the world the way they were. Did climate play a role? What about geology? If so, did one factor have a greater impact than others? Solving these problems would help support Darwin's theory of evolution. Darwin wrote the following to Gray:

> "As I am no Botanist, it will seem so absurd to you my asking botanical questions, that I may premise that I have for several years been collecting facts on 'variation,' and when I find that any general remark seems to hold amongst animals, I try to test it in plants."

Sir Joseph Dalton Hooker, one of the greatest British botanists of the 19th century, had observed and recorded many plant communities in the European Alps and the Arctic that seemed to have similar characteristics. According to Hooker, it was as if the two flora had once shared a single habitat and then been separated. Hooker also happened to be Darwin's closest friend and had actually introduced Darwin and Gray in 1838. Hooker and Darwin had discussed in detail the abnormalities of plant distribution and how they seemed to support Darwin's ideas about how species change.

Darwin had observed species of finches on the Galapagos islands in 1835. He noticed that different species displayed variations in beak shape and size based on diet. Just like the finches, plant species on nearby islands often took closely similar forms. This suggested descent from common ancestors. Hooker knew full well that if Darwin's theory could help Gray solve the North American-east Asian relationship, it would not only strengthen Darwin's theory, but it would win Darwin an important American ally.

In 1857, Darwin wrote Gray a letter which contained an abstract detailing his theory of evolution and his ideas on natural selection. His mechanism seemed simple. Individuals who happen to inherit advantageous traits have a greater chance of surviving and reproducing. Gray eventually solved this problem by treating the two great continents as separate islands that were once fused. We know now about plate tectonics, but this idea during Gray's time was revolutionary. Gray connected and disconnected the two continents with help from Agassiz's Ice Age theory. Gray realized that

Darwin's theory would help him explain the North American-east Asian plant problem if the following were true:

1) North America and Asia were treated as islands that were formerly joined;

2) In the warm part of the Tertiary (65 million - 2 million years ago) period, a single temperate flora had spread unbroken (because of the Bering Strait land bridge) across the northern reaches of Asia and North America;

3) This band of flora lay well north of what later became Japan and eastern North America; and

4) When the next Ice Age came, the cooling climate pushed these plant communities southward, splitting them, as they moved down either side of the Pacific into separate communities in North America and eastern Asia. Climactic changes, such as drying of the American west, then pushed the two communities into more limited areas.

This still did not explain why the plant species in both locations were similar, but not identical. This is where Darwin's theory provided the most support; similar species rose from ancestor species and had diverged over thousands of years in these separated areas.

While studying plant specimens from Japan in 1858, Gray recognized a "familiar" plant. This species from Japan was almost identical to *Shortia galacifolia*, his mystery plant. Even though the Japanese variety had been named already, Gray was confident that it belonged to the *Shortia* genus. Further, Gray had the opportunity to join an expedition in 1877, along with Hooker, to document geography and geology of the Rocky Mountains. Ferdinand Hayden, head of the Rocky Mountain region of the U.S. Geological Survey, led this summer exploration. Hayden had previously directed the first federally funded geological survey into the Yellowstone region in 1871. Gray and Hooker were invited on this trip because of their knowledge of North American and Asian flora. They both concluded that even though there did seem to be a connection between the flora of the eastern U.S. and temperate Asia, this same relationship did not seem to exist with the Rocky Mountain species. This helped Gray cement his ideas on the connections. This find, along with the letters from Hooker and Darwin, convinced Gray that Darwin's ideas could explain the plant problem. This is also why visiting Statesville, NC in 1879 was so fulfilling for Gray.

After teaching his last class at Harvard, Asa Gray devoted most of his time to research, writing and lecturing. Most of his lecturing revolved around promoting Darwin's ideas. In December 1887, Gray experienced paralysis in his arm and lost his ability to speak. He died during the evening of January 30, 1888, at the age of 77.

Charles Darwin went on to become not only one of the most influential scientists but also one of the most influential figures in history. Even though Darwin published many books and papers, he is best known for his book published in 1859, *On the Origins of Species*, which outlined his ideas on evolution by natural selection.

What Darwin, Gray, or anyone else did not fully understand was just how dynamic geology can be in shaping landscapes.

Chapter 3

Something Hotter

–.–.–.–.–

The form of a coast, the configuration of the interior of a country, the existence and extent of lakes, valleys, and mountains, can often be traced to the former prevalence of earthquakes and volcanoes in regions which have long been undisturbed. To these remote convulsions the present fertility of some districts the sterile character of others, the elevation of land above the sea, the climate, and various peculiarities, may be distinctly referred.

- Charles Lyell

DIFFERENT FACTORS CREATE AND REGULATE THE distribution of plant and animal species which help form ecosystems. Geological factors like glaciers are vital to this process. Glaciers were not the sole influencer of the GYE. Something else was, and still is, at play here in the northwest corner of Wyoming. Something hotter.

This ecosystem offers the rare chance for people, not just professional scientists, to immerse themselves in geology. Geology is important because it influences the entire ecosystem by forming the foundation, literally and figuratively. Volcanic and hydrothermal processes along with the previously discussed glacial process help distribute various types of sediment, which allow for certain types of vegetation and ultimately species to establish themselves. Yellowstone's geology is unique because you can see geological processes at work in real time. We now turn our attention to the history of geology as a field of science.

By the late 18th century, scientists knew a lot about Earth. They knew the dimensions of the Earth and even its distance from the sun and other planets. However, determining the age of the Earth would prove to be a difficult task. There were several reasons for this.

First, not many people were studying geology. It was hard for non-scientists, and even some scientists, to become engaged in the field. James Hutton, who is given credit for creating the field of geology, was one of the few enthusiasts. Hutton's downfall was that he was a poor communicator. In 1795, he wrote about the slow processes that shaped the planet, but this writing did little good in advancing the field because, quite frankly, it was boring. The general public could not understand it. Hutton did ask one crucial question: *Why are ancient clamshells and other marine fossils so often found on mountaintops?* He concluded that the marine fossils had risen along with the mountains themselves and also deduced that it was the heat within the Earth that created new rocks and continents. According to Hutton, it was this heat that caused land to erupt from the surface and form mountain chains. The amazing thing is all this conjecture was 200 years before plate tectonics would be adopted as a scientific theory.

Geology did not spark much interest in the U.S. until Charles Lyell, the greatest geologist of the 19th century, gave a series of lectures in Boston in 1841. Lyell had published *The Principles of Geology* in three volumes between 1830-33. Some of Lyell's thoughts and ideas seemed to support Hutton's theories, primarily that the earth was entirely shaped by slow-moving forces that operate even today. This book was so influential that Charles Darwin took a copy of it with him on the Beagle voyage, and used the idea that land changes slowly to adopt a view that living species also have potential to adapt over time. With land, heat had to be a key factor in this change.

Yellowstone National Park (YNP) is an uphill drive in all directions. This is because a supervolcano lurks beneath the park and causes upwellings of molten rock. According to geologist Robert Smith, this volcano is "living, breathing, shaking, and baking."

Geological time is divided into four big chunks known as eras: 1) Precambrian; 2) Paleozoic (541 million years ago); 3) Mesozoic (252 million years ago); and 4) Cenozoic (66 million years ago). The oldest layers deposited in Yellowstone are from the Paleozoic. Dinosaurs roamed much of the Yellowstone area during the Mesozoic. During the Cenozoic, most of the current geological features formed in Yellowstone, including eruptions that covered living trees in ash, mud, and debris.

Within the park, there is a caldera, a depression formed from three major eruptions. The caldera occupies over one-third of the 2.2 million-acre park. The most substantial explosions took place 2.1 million years ago, 1.3 million years ago, and 640,000 years ago. The eruption 2.1 million years ago spilled around 600 cubic miles of ash, which is 2,400 times the amount produced during the 1980 eruption of Mt. St. Helens. The perfect combination of liquids, heat, rock, and movement create enormous potential for eruptions. In fact, there are no more peaks in Yellowstone that stand above 12,000 feet because of these past explosions.

It is helpful to picture Earth as a ball with a central core surrounded by concentric layers. These layers are made up of a lower mantle, an upper mantle, and eventually culminate in the crust. It is about 4,000 miles from the Earth's surface to the center of the core. The mantle is approximately 1,800 miles thick. Above the mantle, the crust is anywhere from three to forty-eight miles thick. The edge of the crust forms the floors of the oceans and the continents. In Yellowstone, basaltic magma begins to form just 125 miles below the Earth's surface because thermal plume heats the upper mantle. This magma flows slowly upward and accumulates in a pie-shaped magma chamber at the base of the crust. The granite that makes up the continental crust next to the magma chamber partially melts and produces a second type of magma called rhyolite. The climax of an eruption is a tremendous outpouring of hot gas, ash, magma, and chunks of rock ripped off walls of the vents. After an eruption such as this, most ejected material falls back and spreads out laterally. Pyroclastic flow refers to this mixture of ash, gas, and rock. This debris from the ash forms a type of rock called tuff.

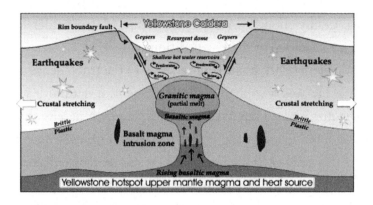

FIG. 3.1. Yellowstone caldera

The thermal features in Yellowstone are holes in the Earth's crust from which hot fluids escape, including water, steam, gases, and vapors. Most of the water in YNP's thermal features comes from rain and snow-melt that percolates into the ground. Hot bedrock in the subsurface heats the water, lowering its density and causing it to circulate back upward to the thermal features at the surface. The water is heated above the boiling point but stays as a liquid because of the tremendous pressure of the overlying rock. The bedrock is heated both by the thermal plume beneath YNP and by rhyolite magma that exists as little as two miles below the surface. In reality, Yellowstone is an enormous pressure cooker, fueled by this supervolcano. Yellowstone has four main thermal features: geysers, hot springs, mud pots, and fumaroles, or steam vents.

It was precisely these bubbling and fiery eruptions that fueled curiosity and caused people to organize trips to see the area. Oddly enough, William Clark and Merriweather Lewis did not lead one of these expeditions.

William Clark was a frontiersman in the truest sense of the word. He was a soldier, an Indian agent, a natural leader, a navigator, and a mapmaker. More than anything else, he was an explorer. Clark, along with Merriweather Lewis, once traveled this part of the country. They saw Paradise Valley just north of the park. They smelled the sage, watched pronghorn and mule deer sprint through the grass, and even slept on the valley floor that was carved by the glacier. They sat by the river, which the Minnetaree people named Mi tsea-da-zi or "Yellow Rock River." In 1805, Lewis and Clark translated it as "Yellow Stone," and the name stuck.

As much as they learned from the American west, Clark decided not to explore the source of the Yellowstone River. Clark even quoted the following in his journal in 1809:

> "At the head of this river the natives give an account that there is frequently heard a loud noise, like thunder, which makes the earth tremble. They state that they seldom go there because their children cannot sleep."

Why wouldn't Clark explore the area further? Just another forty miles south would have revealed some of these magnificent geological features. In July 1806, while Clark was camping close to modern day Livingston, Montana, he decided it would be best to rendezvous with Lewis so that they could make it home before winter. It was a missed opportunity for the expedition. However, one member of their party would decide to go back.

John Colter was allowed to leave the party in August 1806 so that he could continue exploring. Colter was known for his hunting ability, being able to navigate the forests, and being able to make deals with the local Native American tribes. In October 1807, it is widely believed that Colter explored some of the area that now sits in YNP and observed geysers and other thermal features.

Lewis and Clark may have missed the opportunity to see and observe these geothermal features in Yellowstone, but other expeditions followed. In 1871, during the Hayden Expedition, photographs were taken, and paintings were completed to help convince the U.S. Congress that this land should be protected. These photographs showed the beautiful landscape of what appeared to be an alien land. What the pictures and paintings could not show were the intricate and complicated micro-ecosystems that often go unnoticed.

Part Two: Unnoticed Ecosystems

Mammoth Hot Springs. The terrace formations at Mammoth are made of travertine, a type of freshwater limestone.

Chapter 4

Cell Biology Primer

$$-.-.-.-.-.-$$

It is only on the molecular level that we see the living world divide into three distinct primary groups.

- Carl Woese

MOST PEOPLE WHO ENTER YELLOWSTONE'S northern gate under the historic Roosevelt Arch will make the long drive south to see the geothermal features including Grand Prismatic or Old Faithful. Some may drive to the Grand Canyon of the Yellowstone to experience the falls. Others will, no doubt, wander into the Lamar Valley hoping to get a glimpse of wild carnivores. Most will have no idea that just by entering the park, they will be thrust into a world of ancient life-forms. Ancestors of some of these species were among the oldest to inhabit Earth in the deep hydrothermal vents of the oceans. From Gardiner, MT, the closest remnant to the past is located at Mammoth. The historic hotel and visitor center provide visitors with an opportunity to learn about past expeditions to the park. There are old barracks from when the U.S. Army controlled the park. Just south of the hotel, though, there are small microbes that have an older and more interesting story to tell. Let's look at this story.

All living organisms exhibit certain characteristics. These "requirements" unify all of life. For example, organisms are made of cells, can adapt and reproduce, show metabolic behavior, are organized, and grow in some capacity. Cells, the smallest and most basic unit of life, exhibit these characteristics.

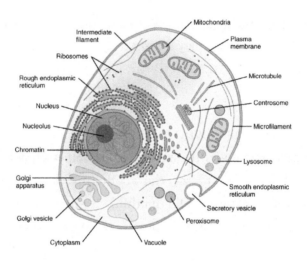

FIG. 4.1. **Eukaryotic cell**

Cells come in different shapes and sizes. Some organisms are single-celled. Others are multi-celled. Life is organized into three main categories, referred to as domains. The three domains of life (Archaea, Prokarya, and Eukarya) are further broken down into kingdoms. The Eukarya domain is what most people know. Eukaryotic cells typically have a nucleus and membrane-bound structures. In a relative sense, eukaryotic cells are more recent cells. Eukaryotic cells make up animals, plants, fungi, and another kingdom full of misfits called protists (i.e., amoeba, paramecia). The Prokaryotic domain contains bacterial cells while single-celled organisms that often live in extreme environments fill the Archaea domain. We will look more into this Archaea group in chapter six. Then, there are particles with which scientists are not quite sure what to do.

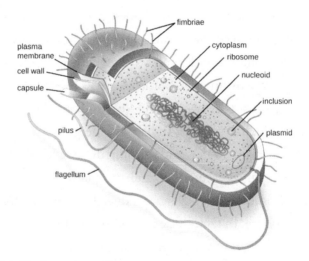

FIG. 4.2. **Prokaryotic cell**

Viruses, not included in any of the domains of life, are genetic information surrounded by a protein capsule. They make up the largest component of biomass on the planet, but whether they qualify as 'bio' represents something of a gray area. We tend to think of the influenza virus or the rhinovirus when we think of viruses because these directly impact us by causing illness. In reality, viruses infect all types of cells. Many are harmless. In fact, most viruses are yet to be discovered. Just like viruses, many smaller, microscopic cells remain mysteries because they are understudied and live in hard to get to places. It may be that these microscopic organisms hold the most secrets for how ecosystems work. This is certainly the case in the thermal features of Yellowstone.

The micro-ecosystems of the geothermal features do contain eukaryotic cells and organisms, but bacteria, archaea, and viruses also that inhabit this area in vast amounts. Since these thermal areas are sometimes extremely hot with an altered pH, learning how microbes survive and thrive can be fascinating. Thermophiles refer to the many microbes that can tolerate hot environments. Some are very closely related to the first life forms that were able to photosynthesize. These cyanobacteria, like plants, can harness energy from the sun and use it to convert water and carbon dioxide to oxygen and sugars. The sugar is used to fuel the plant and also to feed animals. Some of the oxygen produced is released back into the atmosphere. In fact, these early cyanobacteria were the first photosynthesizers around three billion years ago and were responsible for the current atmosphere that supports human life. Not all bacteria in these pools photosynthesize. Some chemosynthesize, which means they harness energy from chemicals instead of light. *Thermus*, a type of bacteria, can go through photosynthesis as well as oxidize arsenic into a non-toxic form.

Archaea, for the most part, live in the most extreme environments. Like bacteria, these microbes are single-celled and have no true nucleus. Unlike bacteria, they have a different outer membrane composition. They are able to survive acidic environments because their tough outer membrane contains enzymes that keep the acid out. One of the most common Archaea found in Yellowstone is *Sulfolobus*. Technically, it is both a thermophile and acidophile, since its ideal environment has a pH between two and three with a temperature of 104-131° F. This unique microbe oxidizes hydrogen sulfide into sulfuric acid, which helps dissolve rock into mud. This is why *Sulfolobus* is found in the hot, acidic, muddy springs of the park. One of the most interesting facts about *Sulfolobus* is that it is parasitized by viruses. The viruses, which cannot survive prolonged exposure to the extreme conditions on their own, seek temporary shelter in *Sulfolobus* to survive and reproduce. These bacteria and archaea tend to hang out at the bottom of the food chain. As we move up the chain, we find some thermophilic eukaryotic organisms.

The protists are a group of eukaryotic microbes that are the most diverse kingdom on Earth. It is almost as if scientists throw all the "unknown" and weird organisms into this group. The thermal pools harbor some of these unique protists. *Vorticella*, a protozoan predator, has been found near the Mammoth area. This tiny microbe is shaped like an inverted bell and lives in water rich in decaying organic matter where it feeds on thermophilic bacteria. *Naegleria*, a type of amoeba that eats bacteria, has also been collected near the Mammoth area. One particular species, *N. fowleri*, lives in warm water, and if inhaled through the nose can enter a human brain. The microbe then uses brain matter as a food source. These microbes, along with their viral inhabitants, are part of the intricate micro-food web. There are also animals involved. For that, we will turn our attention to a relationship between a mite and a small fly.

Chapter 5

Fire Flies

— . — . — . — . —

Flies will not land on a boiling pot.

- Anonymous

Organisms often hitch rides. They do this for a variety of reasons. Some need to conserve energy. Others prefer to get to their destination more efficiently. For some, maybe it's to get away from a predator. The parasitic water mite, *Partnuniella thermals*, just needs to survive.

These mites live in the hydrothermal areas of Yellowstone, specifically on algal-bacterial mats, and use brine flies (Diptera: Ephydridae) as hosts. In Yellowstone, there are three large species of brine flies that feed and lay eggs on the hydrothermal mats. *Ephyrdra thermophila* live in the acidic thermal areas, *Ephydra bruesi* thrive in low-productive alkaline areas, and *Paracoenia turbida* inhabit the highly productive alkaline pools. All three seem to be vehicles for the red mites.

The algal-bacterial mats drive the relationship between parasite (mite) and host (fly). When the mats are young and thin, they are not accessible to the flies because they are covered by hot water. As time passes and the mats grow, exceed the water level, and then divert water flow. The mats cool to below 104° F as they are exposed to the air. This cooling gives the flies just enough time to land, feed, and lay eggs. As the larvae hatch they immediately begin feeding on the mats, which causes the mats to lose their thickness and dip back below the water. Adults or un-emerged larvae that overstay their welcome on the mats are washed out. This provides a continuous cycle of growth and regrowth for the mats, but also requires a window of perfect timing for the flies.

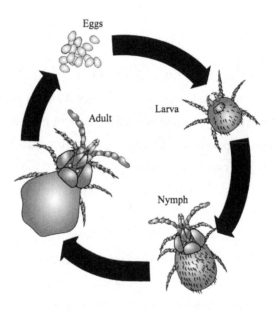

FIG. 5.1. **Mite life cycle**

Like the flies, the mites also lay their eggs on the mats. These eggs hatch into parasitic larvae that strategically jump onto the bodies of flies as they walk by. The flies may groom themselves and remove the mites. Occasionally, though, a mite will go unnoticed and remain attached where it will begin to feed on the fly until the fly dies. The mite will then detach, enter the water, and later emerge as a nymph where it will feed on fly eggs as an adult.

The unique thing about this mite's behavior is that it is only parasitic during the larval stage. Some of the mite's closest relatives have extended their parasitic lifestyle into the nymph stage. Others have entirely done away with the parasitic lifestyle. Biologists believe the explanation of this particular mite's behavior lies in the hot spring environment.

Other mites that extend their parasitic lifestyle must attach to adult flies and feed on the flies for several weeks. *Partnuniella* uses flies of all ages because it does not have multiple weeks to feed. The opportunity window is narrow. *Partnuniella* can only afford to stay attached to the host fly for five to six days.

The greatest risk of death in *Partnuniella*'s life cycle occurs during the transition from egg to parasitic larva. As much as 90% of the larvae never attach to a host fly and, eventually, die on the mat. So, why not abandon parasitism altogether? *Partnuniella* needs the host fly as an energy source and as a means of dispersal. Without the ability to disperse, the mite would go extinct. Adult mites, as well as nymphs, feed on fly eggs. Since these eggs are only laid on the mats that are above water at a particular time and place, the parasitic mite larvae need to get to those spots. In an unstable environment like hot springs where the water flow is not predictable, dispersal is important.

This does not explain how *Partnuniella*, as a population, deals with the loss of 90% of its larvae. How does it survive from generation to generation? Adult mites have the remarkable ability to store large amounts of energy for long periods of time. Experiments have shown that the adults can survive for three months without food in a laboratory. This fits their lifestyle since the exposed mats (and feeding areas) are continually changing. Storing energy over long periods allows them not only to survive as individuals but also to reproduce continuously over long periods. The more they reproduce, the more likely some larvae will survive.

Through years and years of adaptations, natural selection has orchestrated this relationship in such a way that the parasitic water mite is suited to its environment. Often the smallest organisms have the most unique stories to tell. Unfortunately, this minuscule world usually goes unnoticed.

As is always the case, we humans want to know what is in it for us, as if studying for curiosity's sake is not enough. The hot springs in Yellowstone can claim at least one life-altering advancement for humans. Again, we just have to be willing to listen to the story.

Chapter 6

Ancient Benefits

‾.‾.‾.‾.‾.‾

If I could do it all over again, and relive my vision in the twenty-first century, I would be a microbial ecologist. Ten billion bacteria live in a gram of ordinary soil, a mere pinch held between thumb and forefinger. They represent thousands of species, almost none of which are known to science. Into that world I would go with the aid of modern microscopy and molecular analysis.

- E.O. Wilson, *Naturalist*

THERE'S VERY LITTLE A SMALL TOWN CAN DO TO prepare for what Narborough, England experienced in the 1980s. Within three years, Narborough dealt with two horrific homicides. On November 21, 1983, fifteen-year-old Linda Mann left her house to walk to a friend's house. She never made it home. The following day, her body was found just off a deserted footpath. Mann had been strangled and raped. On July 31, 1986, Dawn Ashworth, also fifteen, went missing. Authorities determined that Ashworth was walking home when she decided to use a footpath as a shortcut. Her body was also found with signs indicating she had been strangled and raped. The families were devastated. The community was in shock.

Richard Buckland, an employee at the nearby psychiatric hospital, quickly became the prime suspect in both cases. He knew details of Ashworth's body. While being questioned, Buckland admitted to the killing of Ashworth. He, however, denied killing Mann in 1983. The police thought he was lying and wanted to find a way to prove that Buckland had committed both murders.

The detectives turned to Dr. Alec Jeffreys, a geneticist at the University of Leicester. Jeffreys had a "eureka" moment in 1984 as he was looking at an 'x-ray' image of DNA samples from an employee and the employee's family. He noticed both differences and similarities between the family members' DNA. He soon realized the scope and potential of this DNA "fingerprinting" and how it could be used for identification purposes. In 1985, Jeffreys used his method to solve an immigration case. Jeffreys was reluctant to try this process in a double homicide case, but he decided to use the evidence. Authorities in Narborough could not believe the results. According to the DNA testing, neither murder matched with Richard Buckland. This case was the first time that DNA evidence was used to drop all charges against an innocent man.

The police finally made an arrest in 1987. The suspect's DNA matched the crime scenes, leaving him no choice but to confess to both homicides. DNA testing is now used for far more than just immigration and homicide cases.

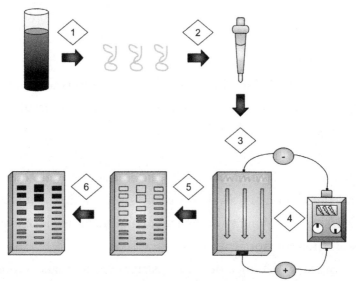

FIG. 6.1. **Gel electrophoresis is a process where an electrical current is applied to DNA samples.** 1) DNA is extracted; 2) DNA is isolated and amplified; 3) DNA is added to the gel; 4) Electric current is applied to the gel; 5) DNA bands are separated by size; and 6) DNA bands are stained.

Deoxyribonucleic acid, also known as DNA, is the genetic compound of living organisms that provides the code for the cells to make proteins. It is made up of carbon, hydrogen, oxygen, nitrogen, and phosphorous at the most basic level. These elements construct the three main parts of the DNA molecule: a phosphate group, a deoxyribose sugar, and one of four possible nitrogen base groups. These four nitrogen bases, which are represented by the letters *A, T, C,* and *G,* represent the code of DNA. The letters are consistent across all of life.

In the early 1950s, the structure of DNA was found to be a double helix. Think about two linear structures attached by horizontal bonds just like the rungs of a ladder. Then imagine you twist that ladder like a spiral staircase, and you will have a pretty good picture of the structure of this tiny molecule. The letters, or code, are found on those rungs facing inside. We also know that the strands of a DNA molecule fit together in a specific way. The *A* always pairs and forms a bond with the *T*, and the *C* with the *G*. The variations in number and size of DNA strands along with the letter combinations make organisms different from each other.

Since DNA includes the instructions to make proteins necessary for the body, it is essential that DNA molecules get replicated within a cell before the cell divides. In multicellular organisms, cell division provides for growth and replacement of cells, but also for reproduction of the organism. This is how genetic information gets passed to offspring. Each cell is equipped with molecular machinery to replicate the DNA. For that to happen, each strand in the double helix must break apart. Each *A* and *T* must break bonds as well as each *C* and *G*. Molecular scissors called polymerase molecules are responsible for this break. DNA testing and analyses require these polymerase molecules.

Let's delve into how the DNA testing process works and why it matters. For that, we must go back to the 1950s and look at how a simple discovery in Yellowstone triggered a $300 million per year industry.

After completing his Ph.D. in 1952, Thomas Brock took a position in the antibiotics research department at Upjohn

Company in Michigan, where he became self-taught in microbiology out of necessity. From 1965 to 1975, Brock conducted field and laboratory research, funded by the National Science Foundation, on thermophilic microorganisms in Yellowstone National Park. Temperature is one of the most important environmental factors, and organisms differ in their ability to adapt to it. Of the three major domains of life (Eukarya, Bacteria, and Archaea), organisms that fall within the Archaea have been shown to have the ability to withstand a tremendous amount of heat. Therefore, they are often referred to as thermophiles. For comparison, the figure below shows the upper-temperature limits for certain organisms.

Eukarya

Fish	100° F
Insects	122° F
Vascular plants	113° F
Mosses	122° F
Algae	140° F
Fungi	144° F

Bacteria

Cyanobacteria	163° F
Heterotrophic bacteria	194° F

Archaea

Methanogens	230° F
Sulfur-dependent	239° F

FIG. 6.2. The upper-temperature limits among the three domains.

Water boils in Yellowstone at around 198° F, so both bacteria and archaea are thriving in hot temperatures. In 1969, Thomas Brock and his graduate student reported that they had isolated an organism from a sample of pink bacteria collected from Mushroom Spring in Yellowstone. This organism, which they named *Thermus aquaticus*, was living at 160° F.

In 1983, Dr. Kary Mullis invented a method of amplifying, or making a copy of, any DNA region. He did this through repeated cycles of duplication driven by an enzyme called DNA polymerase. This enzyme would be key. The process is known as polymerase chain reaction or PCR. Dr. Mullis was awarded the Nobel Prize in Chemistry in 1993 for this discovery.

At the core of the PCR method is the use of a suitable DNA polymerase, a protein enzyme, that can withstand the high temperatures required for separation of the two DNA strands in the double helix after each replication cycle. *Taq* polymerase, a DNA polymerase from *Thermus aquaticus*, was perfectly suited to do this. It is stable at high temperatures, and it remains active even after DNA denaturation. Remember that is the exact environment it was found in by Thomas Brock and his students.

This set the stage for trying to solve the footpath murders in England. DNA fingerprinting uses variations in the genetic code to identify individuals. PCR is one of the initial steps to DNA analysis simply because the DNA needs to be amplified, or copied. This profiling has wide-scale applications, including paternity cases, criminal cases, immigration disputes, family history, and wildlife population studies.

Beyond biotechnology, sometimes the unnoticed organisms and their relationships drive the ecosystem dynamics of larger animals. In some cases, predators and prey animals are just the puppets with tiny parasitic worms acting as the puppeteer.

Chapter 7

If You Give a Moose a Tapeworm

At some unknown moment, the moose's spirit passed, and the spirit of the pack was renewed. This miracle of life and death occurs several times a week on Isle Royale.

- John Vucetich

WITH LITTLE DAYLIGHT LEFT, JOHN VUCETICH AND his pilot, Dan Glaser, noticed a bull moose feeding at the edge of a forest. Instead of passing by in the small plane, they decided to make several passes to keep an eye on the bull. John and Dan needed to check on several local wolf packs from the air. John, an ecologist, is the leader of the longest running predator-prey study on Isle Royale, a remote island isolated by Lake Superior. He took over as the head scientist from Rolf Peterson. This particular study focuses on wolf and moose relationships. Dan splits his time between flying for Isle Royale winter aerial surveys and piloting in rough Alaskan terrain.

Minutes before seeing the moose, John and Dan had seen a pack of wolves. They thought that if they watched long enough, they might have the opportunity to observe a conflict. The wolves and moose eventually saw one another, but not until they were fifty meters apart. The moose immediately fled, which caused the wolves to go into attack mode. They quickly caught up to the massive bull and soon found themselves at his heels. This part of the chase is dangerous for the much smaller canine. One hoof to the head could be fatal.

The bull turned around to face the pack. The pack then stopped and surrounded him. The wolves took turn lunging towards his rear as the he tried to do the impossible and face each wolf at the same time. Once again, the moose attempted to flee by breaking open the circle of wolves. One wolf bit the back of the moose and held on for a ride. Then another bit down. Then two more latched on and would not let go. The combined strength of the four wolves managed to bring down the back of the moose. However, his front remained upright. After forty minutes, the wolves managed to completely bring him down. John later reported, "As the once powerful and magnificent body of this bull moose hit the ground, all eight wolves struck the moose and began tearing its flesh from all sides."

Patrick Endrews, a wildlife photographer from Alaska, made a similar observation as he was leaving Denali National Park late one evening. He came across a cow moose defending her calf from a lone wolf. The cow had backed into the shallow part of a river with the calf behind her while the wolf stood on the bank. Within minutes, five more wolves came and took turns lunging at her, desperately trying to get to the calf. The wolves dodged death several times before they eventually got the calf and dragged it away. Their determination paid off.

What John, Dan, and Patrick witnessed was nature in its rawest form. How typical is this behavior, though? Some moose stand seven feet and weigh 1500 pounds. You wouldn't think wolves would bring down these gigantic creatures often. Attempting to kill a moose comes with plenty of risks like having skulls crushed by hooves or bodies pierced by antlers. Under the right circumstances, wolves can avoid danger. They certainly must possess plenty of skills, but luck is also a factor.

According to the Yellowstone Wolf Project Annual Report 2012, researchers detected 255 kills made by wolves during the year. Of those, only two were confirmed moose. Compare that number with 159 elk, and you realize that it must be easier to take down an elk. Wolves in Yellowstone do not have anything to gain from hunting moose when there are plenty of elk. However, wolves that live in areas with only moose as prey must be careful. One strategy is to wait until the moose is already in trouble. For example, winter may be an ideal time to find a moose in peril because of the lack of food and depth of snow. The energy demands are sometimes too high for the moose. Snowy conditions may not be the only factor that contributes to an energy-depleted moose. According to some research, the wolves may be getting help from an unexpected source.

Echinococcus granulosis, a type of tapeworm, hails from the phylum Platyhelminthes and class Cestoda and is a common larval parasite of moose. Wolves and other canines serve as definitive hosts. How could tapeworms no longer than five millimeters help wolves hunt moose more efficiently? It is important to understand the life cycle of this tapeworm to properly answer this question. *E. granulosis* live as adults in the intestines of wolves where they produce eggs. These tapeworm eggs contain an embryo called an oncosphere, or hexcanth. This embryo has six tiny hooklets. The outside portion of the egg protects the embryo during its journey. These eggs eventually pass through the wolf in the feces.

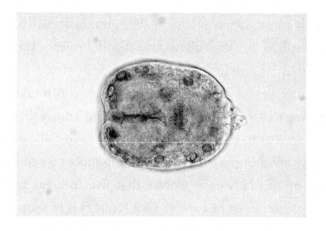

FIG. 7.1. *E. granulosis* **has an anterior end called the scolex.** This is a specialized body segment that anchors the parasite to the host.

Moose accidentally ingest these eggs as they graze on vegetation. The eggs hatch inside the small intestine of the moose, release the embryos, then the embryos penetrate the intestinal wall (remember the hooklets?) and invade the circulatory system of the moose. From here, the embryos enter organs, such as the liver and lungs, where they develop into cysts. Each cyst grows from the inside and can get quite large.

To complete the life cycle of *E. granulosis*, wolves become infected again after consuming the moose organs.

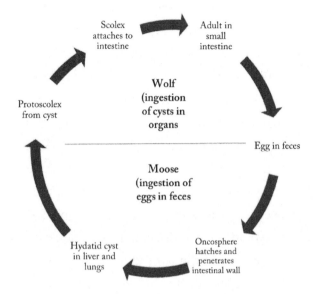

FIG. 7.2. *E. granulosis* **requires two hosts.** Wolves consume the cysts in the moose organs. In turn, the moose consume the eggs in feces.

The tapeworm does not seem to negatively impact the wolves. However, the cysts that grow in the moose cause problems. Some researchers think that these cysts leave the moose more susceptible to predation by wolves because they form and grow in the lungs. It would make sense that a lung infection in an individual moose would make it an easy target for a wolf, especially if that moose is already struggling due to difficult environmental conditions. Two researchers devised some fascinating methods to test this idea. They stated that if *E. granulosis* did increase moose vulnerability to wolf predation, then they should be able to tell by looking at the concentration of tapeworms across a moose population. Highly concentrated tapeworms in an area mean that few individual moose harbor most of the parasitic worms. In a moose population that experiences high predation pressure from wolves, the distribution of these parasites should be less concentrated and more evenly distributed than in a moose population with low predation pressure. The research supported this hypothesis and can easily be explained.

In an area where many wolves actively hunt moose, one would expect that those moose that are highly infected with tapeworms would be at a disadvantage. They may be slower and weaker because of the large cysts in their lungs. Once the wolves kill the highly infected moose, only the moose that have a lesser concentration of the parasites, or none at all, would be left. However, in an area where there are low numbers of wolves hunting moose, the parasitic tapeworms would be found in higher concentrations. Those moose with bad infections would not be weeded out of a population as fast because of the lack of active predators.

Unanswered Questions 7.1
1. Could parasites control relationships in ecosystems?
2. Are moose and wolves just pawns in this parasitic game of natural selection?

It seems like these tapeworms rely on predator/prey interactions, but it may also be possible that the presence of *E.*

granulosis is necessary for a healthy wolf population in some areas. Maybe the tapeworms, wolves, and moose should all be considered as partners in a healthy functioning ecosystem. In the next section, we will explore some of these unforeseen partnerships.

Part Three: Unexpected Partnerships

Fallen lodgepole pine tree with cones nearby. Lodgepoles rely on environmental factors and partnerships to thrive in Yellowstone.

Chapter 8

Endosymbiosis Primer

−.−.−.−.−.−

Can we think of a good reason why one cell getting inside another cell should transform the prospects of prokaryotes, unleashing the potential of eukaryotic complexity? Yes. There is a compelling reason, and it relates to energy.

-Nick Lane, The Vital Question

IN THE BIOLOGICAL REALM, PARTNERSHIPS WERE always bound to happen. Symbiosis is the term that is used to define 'living together.' Some of these associations are bad for both parties, some are good for both, some are neutral, and some benefit one while harming the other. Wherever and whatever the situation, these relationships are sometimes necessary. As we look through the natural history of organisms, we see a pattern of partnerships develop, from the subcellular level and how structures came to live inside of cells all the way to the ecological community level and how populations of organisms interact with each other. We will highlight several relationships that we see in biology, and show examples of how some of these impact Yellowstone's flora and fauna.

Lynn Margulis grew up in Chicago during the 1940s with three younger sisters. She earned an undergraduate degree from the University of Chicago when she was eighteen. There she met the famous astronomer Carl Sagan, whom she later married. At twenty-two years of age, she finished a graduate degree in genetics and zoology. Little did anyone realize at the time that Margulis would eventually become a trailblazing biological theorist. Soon after completing a Ph.D. in 1965, she attempted to get a manuscript published which outlined her theory of endosymbiosis. It was rejected fifteen times before finally being accepted by the *Journal of Theoretical Biology*. This article showed how chloroplasts and mitochondria found themselves inside of cells. Endosymbiosis is a landmark theory in biology. Margulis expanded this paper into her first book, *Origin of Eukaryotic Cells*.

Eukaryotic cells, the basic units of plants, animals, fungi, and protists, have many unique adaptations. You would be hard-pressed to find a modification more impressive, or needed, than the ability to both break down food through a series of chemical reactions and use oxygen to produce energy units called adenosine triphosphate, or ATP. This process, called aerobic cellular respiration, harnesses energy from the sugar we eat. Organisms rely on ATP for many vital functions such as transporting nutrients across cell membranes, contracting and relaxing muscles in animals, and powering the motors that move sperm cells. Many day-to-day chemical reactions use this energy molecule.

Food (glucose) + Oxygen → Carbon dioxide + Water + ATP (energy)

FIG. 8.1. **The process of cell respiration takes place in mitochondria.** ATP, which fuels the cell and organism, is one of the products.

The production of ATP would not be possible without structures called mitochondria that live inside eukaryotic cells. These mitochondria, sometimes called the 'powerhouses' of the cell, can harness and extract most of the stored up energy inside a glucose molecule so that the cell can perform tasks that allow it to not only stay alive but also to thrive. For example, when an animal inhales oxygen, red blood cells pick up the oxygen molecules and carry them throughout the body. Oxygen then diffuses into cells. The mitochondria in those cells use this oxygen to finish the steps of cell respiration and make the majority of ATP for the body. Our muscle cells would pause in a state of anaerobic respiration without mitochondria. If you have ever exercised, chances are you have experienced soreness, cramping, or muscle failure that are all consequences of muscles running low on oxygen. If it were not for mitochondria, we would not be able to function.

Food is key. Some organisms, like humans, obtain food by eating. Others make their food. Plants, and even some non-plants, photosynthesize. Tiny structures called chloroplasts trap light energy from the sun and use it to make glucose. Chloroplasts contain the pigment chlorophyll which gives plants their green color.

| Water + Carbon dioxide + Light → Food (glucose) + Oxygen |

FIG. 8.2. **The process of photosynthesis takes place in chloroplasts.** Photosynthesis allows organisms, like plants, to make food.

Mitochondria and chloroplasts are different than most other cellular structures; they have their own set of unique DNA. Most of a cell's DNA that is translated into proteins and give us specific characteristics is found in the nucleus. Why then would mitochondria and chloroplasts need a separate set of genetic information? Does this tell us anything about their origin?

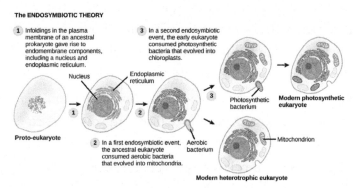

FIG. 8.3. **Endosymbiotic Theory**

Margulis provided evidence that suggested mitochondria and chloroplasts once lived independently from a cell. Once they found their way into a cell, like an animal or plant cell, the partnership was too good to pass up. Plant and animal cells are much larger than mitochondria and chloroplasts and thus gave them a safe place to reside. The cell provided protection. In turn, the mitochondria provided the cell with plentiful ATP molecules, and the chloroplasts provided some cells with food. This relationship is the perfect example of mutualism, where both parties benefit from the relationship. If we move several steps up from the cellular level to organisms, we see another mutualistic relationship that has developed between two land-dwellers.

Chapter 9

Lichen this Relationship

–.–.–.–.–

There is a low mist in the woods— It is a good day to study lichens.
- Henry David Thoreau

NO ONE MADE CHASING DOWN ANCIENT artifacts cooler than Indiana Jones. He would leave the safety of his classroom, which required battling bad guys, to track down objects. Fortunately for us, all we have to do is step outside to be in the midst of something much more primitive than anything Dr. Jones collected. Step out, and you will quickly find yourself in the presence of a species from another age. It surrounds us, but we rarely notice it. Some researchers even think it may have also laid the foundation for terrestrial life. It's not just one species. It's two different species intertwined as one, creating various colors and structures.

Lichen is a symbiotic relationship between two partner species. The mycobiont partner is a fungus that gives struc-ture. Fungi are made up of eukaryotic cells, meaning the internal structure is made up of organized compartments and also a membrane-bound nucleus that stores and protects the delicate genetic code. As such, fungi are heterotrophic organ-isms, obtaining their nutrients externally. In the case of fungi, the process of decomposition acquires food in the form of fixed carbon. If not through decay, the fungus must get the required carbon through a symbiotic relationship with a partner.

A photobiont is the second partner in this relationship. Either green algae or cyanobacteria can fulfill the needs of the fungus because they can both photosynthesize. Green algae belong to the plant kingdom and cyanobacteria is a prokaryotic organism, so they are not even closely related. However, they both make food in the form of glucose, which is the carbon source. This relationship works out well for the fungus. The photobiont provides an endless supply of glucose, and in return, the fungus maintains structure and protection. This partnership may have set the stage for two important events.

Results from a 2001 study revealed that early plants and fungi played a significant role in manipulating the environment in such a way that global glaciation and the evolution of land animals both took place. Photosynthesis, presumably from the photobiont partner, was a major player because it took up carbon dioxide, thus lowering atmospheric levels. At the same time, atmospheric oxygen levels increased.

In this particular paper, researchers tried to determine when plants and fungi colonized the land. Earlier studies had concluded that both came on land about 480 million years ago. Before that, only rocks and bacteria covered the ground. One academic textbook states, "But it was only within the last 500 million years that small plants, fungi, and animals joined them (bacteria) ashore." The 2001 study, however, concluded that plants colonized land 700 million years ago and fungi around 1300 million years ago. These earlier dates are significant because this would mean that plants and fungi became terrestrial during the Precambrian, the oldest geological eon. If land fungi and plants did appear during the Precambrian, how could they have played a role in both ice age events and the explosion of various animal forms that we see in the fossil record?

Before we understand the role they played, we need to know how hard it is to live on land. Compared with living in the water, or at least near water, plants need to have specific structures like roots, stems and leaves to transport water and sugars. Some plants benefit from having a thick waxy layer on leaves to keep too much water from escaping. Living on land is tough, and it would have been especially tricky 700 million years ago. This is where lichens come into the picture.

The terrestrial plants and fungi were not living separately during this early time; they were living in this lichen relationship. This is how they were able to live in the rugged conditions. Lichens are found in harsh places like the Arctic, deserts, and in ecosystems sitting above super volcanoes like Yellowstone. The can live without rain for months. Early in Earth's history, fungi provided the protection that the green algae needed. Photosynthesis could then begin to operate on a massive scale. Carbon dioxide levels in the atmosphere decreased and oxygen levels increased.

When carbon dioxide levels decrease, global temperatures drop. Photosynthesis probably was the main reason why Earth experienced global glaciation events from 750 million years ago to 580 million years ago. This period lines right up with the appearance of lichens and early land plants like mosses.

There may have been other explanations for the decreased carbon dioxide levels. One may have been the mosses and old land plants made up of lignin. Lignin is a tough organic compound that does not readily decompose. Carbon gets 'locked' up in the lignin and cannot get out. This ends up eventually producing fossil fuels if the plant material gets buried over years and years. Another explanation of decreased of carbon dioxide levels is that the first lichens may have produced acids which dissolved the rocks on which they were living. This acid released calcium from the foundation. When calcium is washed away, calcium carbonate limestone forms, which prevents carbon atoms from forming carbon dioxide in the atmosphere.

There was an increase in atmospheric oxygen during the Neoproterozoic era, right before what scientists refer to as the Cambrian explosion. Early in the Cambrian period, some 530 million years ago, a large variety of invertebrate animals inhabited the Earth's oceans. In fact, from 535 million years ago to 525 million years ago, the oldest fossils of nearly half of all extant animal phyla have been found, including the first arthropods, chordates, echinoderms, and the precursor organisms to vertebrates. The lichens and the mosses may have been responsible for this oxygen increase that led to this evolution boom of animals. According to another study, the soil had only been around for the last 450 million years ago. If this is true, this lichen relationship is genuinely older than dirt.

Experts have identified close to 200 lichen relationships in Yellowstone. Several thrive throughout the dry rock-grassland areas while others are found associated with arctic, alpine, and boreal plants. There is a relatively lower diversity of lichens in Yellowstone most likely because of the altitude, dry climate, and the most frequent fires occurring in the lodgepole forests. These lodgepoles just happen to be our next subject.

Chapter 10

Hot Pines, a Fungus, and a Beetle

 ‒.‒.‒.‒.‒.‒

…this is Nature's process for removing the dead of the forest family and for bettering conditions for the living.

- G. L. Hoxie

SMOKEY BEAR HAS BEEN PREVENTING FOREST FIRES since 1944. His advertising statements have ranged from "Smokey Says – Care Will Prevent 9 out of 10 Forest Fires" to "Remember… Only YOU Can Prevent Forest Fires." It would be safe to say that because of the long-running campaign, most people know about Smokey and his fire prevention message.

This emblem and campaign may have been counterproductive. There is no question that Smokey Bear has prevented forest fires, but the promotion has seemed to ignore the benefits of fires. Ecosystems like Yellowstone that are dominated by lodgepole pine trees (*Pinus contorta*) need occasional fires. Suppressed fires could put ecosystems like this in harm's way.

Lodgepoles make both male and female cones. In all conifers, pollen fills the male cones. Unfortunately, most of us know pollen all too well. We have seen the yellow substance stuck on cars and sidewalks. It fills our noses and eyes causing allergic reactions. Ideally, the pollen grains from the male cones make it to the female cones for fertilization. In some conifers, once the female cone is fertilized and reaches maturity, the cone opens, and the seeds are released. The seeds either rely on the wind or animals for dispersal. In lodgepoles, the female cones usually remain closed after maturity. The cones produce a thick resin that binds the cone scales together and rely on heat to release the seeds. When the cones are subjected to temperatures upwards of 122° F, the resin bonds break, and the cone explodes releasing seeds everywhere in a process called serotiny. The cones need heat for propagation, and fire provides this heat.

Lodgepoles dominate Yellowstone. They prefer slightly acidic soils, and because of the horizontal growth of their trunks, they can proliferate in areas that are impacted by fires. This soil preference makes them suitable to Yellowstone because of the shallow topsoil and also because of the caldera that sits beneath. Lodgepoles can quickly grow as a thick forest, but for seeds to establish, they need sunlight. The canopy must open. Fires certainly help with this, but heat is not the only factor that thins out lodgepole forests. There is a complicated web of dependent interactions.

Besides lodgepole pines and fire, two others play in this game: a fungal pathogen and a beetle. *Phaeolus schweinitzii* is a fungus that attacks the roots and the lower trunk portion of conifers. This fungal attack leaves the tree with a weak tree base, which can make it more susceptible to attacks from insects. The mountain pine beetle, *Dendroctonus ponderosae*, is native to western North America and relies on the dead or dying wood. Female beetles chew through the bark to reach the phloem (sugar-carrying vessel) of the tree, where they can find sugar and nutrients. It typically takes one full year for the beetle to complete a life cycle from egg to larva to pupa to adult.

We have established that fire helps with the dispersal of the lodgepole seeds, fungi deter growth and weaken trees, and beetles finish off the trees and, therefore, thin the lodgepole forests. How, exactly, do these factors relate, intertwine, and even depend on each other?

Ecologists surveyed eight different lodgepole forest locations to attempt to determine the relationship. The researchers found that the older pines showed the presence of two essential things. First, old pines were the only ones that had fire scars. One can deduce that these old trees were the only ones that had experienced a fire. Second, these mature trees also showed the presence of a fungal infection. Some between the ages of 30 and 100 years even showed an advanced disease. Mountain pine beetles are more likely to attack the older trees, especially ones infected over an extended period. There is some thought that the fungus acts as a tattletale by signaling to the beetles that specific trees are susceptible. The fungus makes a chemical called trans-verbenol that pine bark beetles can recognize and then attack in mass.

It just so happens that these older, and presumably larger lodgepoles, benefit the beetle population. Beetles typically attack these more massive trees, possibly because they have fire scars and fungal infestations. However, gaining access to more food may be another reason why beetles chose the towering trees. Attacking a small tree could be disastrous because small trees have thin phloem. Less food means a decreased yearly brood for the beetle.

The beetles ultimately kill the old lodgepoles. The wood decomposes, and the nutrients are returned to the soil to aid the germination and growth of new lodgepoles from seeds scattered during the fire. This renewal sets the stage for another set of trees that will grow and mature, disperse seeds after a fire, be susceptible to fungi, then be destroyed by beetles. It all starts with fire. Fires influence ecosystems.

Lodgepoles are not the only pine tree impacted by the mountain pine beetle. The whitebark pine, *Pinus albicaulis*, is also susceptible to beetle infestations. Visitors often overlook the whitebark for two reasons. One, the observer is typically gasping for air when he walks by because of the high altitude. Second, there are not many mature whitebarks left in the GYE. Beetles, along with other factors, are squeezing the whitebark from its historical range and creating a nightmare scenario for the high altitude ecosystem.

Whitebark pine trees in Yellowstone not only form the foundation of the high altitude areas but are also considered a keystone species. They are wind-resistant, can grow in nutrient-poor soil, and also provide food for animals. The problem is that it takes a long time for one individual tree to produce a nut. In typical pine trees, it takes two years to create a cone entirely, but in whitebarks, it may take thirty years to start generating cones, and then another thirty to seventy years to reach full cone-producing potential. A thirty-year gap in cone production would have a devastating impact on the environment.

Red squirrels forage constantly. They are proficient at cutting down cones and caching them away in middens, underground hiding spots. The squirrels also do a pretty good job of defending these burial sites against other small vertebrates. Clark's nutcrackers, a bird member of the Corvidae family, also partake in this meal by collecting cones, eating the nuts, and storing them for later use. The stored nuts that do not get retrieved have the potential to germinate. That is unless a grizzly bear gets to them first.

The whitebark pine nut is vital to the grizzly bear. This nut contains a high-fat content and, therefore, is one of the most significant parts of a bear's fall diet, if available. When bears are feeding on whitebarks it is beneficial to many other animals, including humans, because the bears stay in the high altitude ecosystems. When grizzly bears are eating high on the slopes they are away from more developed areas. You don't want to have hungry grizzlies in and around neighborhoods. If the whitebark pines disappear, it could mean bad news for the already threatened grizzly. Unless, of course, there is something else that the bears could eat while visiting high altitude ecosystems.

Chapter 11

More than a Snack

— · — · — · — · — · —

First we eat, then we do everything else.

- M. F. K. Fisher

THERE ARE BENEFITS TO BEING PROFICIENT reproduc-ers. Individual females of the army cutworm moth (*Euxoa auxiliaries*) can settle into the soil and oviposit, or lay, any-where from 1000 to 3000 eggs. This release of eggs marks the end of a long, spectacular journey for adult moths. Soon after laying the eggs, the adults will die. However, they may die sooner.

Yellowstone contains populations of ungulates, including elk, bison, bighorn sheep, mule and white-tailed deer, pronghorn, mountain goats, and moose. All of these would make an excellent feast for an adult grizzly bear. There's a problem, though. Mountain goats and bighorn sheep can escape to cliffs. These cliffs and their narrow passageways are not forgiving to a lumbering bear. Elk and deer are just fast enough to get away from a charging grizzly most of the time. Pronghorn are way too speedy. Even the fittest grizzly would use a tremendous amount of energy chasing one of these. Moose and bison are too large. If grizzlies were to rely on any of these animals as their primary prey, the risks would be too high. The calves of these ungulates are an option, but they are only available from May to the end of June. Grizzlies are more opportunistic feeders when it comes to ungulate carcasses. They must rely on a hard winter or wolves to create opportunities. Grizzlies prefer food with a lower risk factor; enter the moths in the late summer months.

Also called miller moths, because their wings make dust like the clothes of one who works in a mill, army cutworm moths typically range in length from one to two inches and have an average wingspan between one and two inches. They are holometabolous, meaning they go through complete metamorphism. This includes four stages of development: embryo, larva, pupa, and adult. Having different juvenile and adult forms allows the army cutworm moth to occupy different ecological niches.

These moths overwinter as larvae in the Midwestern states. In the spring, they begin feeding on plants such as alfalfa and smaller grains. Pupation occurs underground after a total of six to seven stages of development from egg to the last molt. Adults emerge in early June and migrate west into the Rocky Mountains. It is this migration that is quite phenomenal and has left researchers scratching their heads.

Presumably, the moths migrate to avoid the high summer temperatures. They also tend to migrate upward in altitude as they seek sources of energy-rich nectar. This increase in elevation leaves them exposed to intense sunlight. It also puts them in the same ecological space as grizzly bears, which make the trip to higher elevations during the warm summer months.

Because of the intense sunlight, the moths will feed on flower nectar at night and hide in dark crevices during the day. These dark cracks are usually underneath the piles of rocks. The bears will dig through and flip over these large rocks to expose and eat the moths. While hiding during the day, the moths will metabolically transform the nectar into fat and increase their body fat by 60% over just one summer. Therefore, the moths are extremely important to grizzlies during the summer and early fall months.

Research studies have shown that the high slopes of southeastern Yellowstone contain high concentrations of moths. Researchers in one particular study counted 470 bears roaming around twenty-nine different moth aggregation sites. In one season alone, 220 individual bears were observed at the sites. This included nineteen females and their cubs. This is odd behavior because grizzlies, especially sows, should not tolerate each other in the late summer months in such proximity. They do it here because there is plenty of food. One observer compared the moth sites to bears at a salmon stream where the bears could not help but eat. In fact, some bears were seen digging whiles moths were flying all around even landing on the bears' arms at times. All the bears would have to do is take a break from excavating to lick their forearms.

Moths do not take cover individually, but in aggregations by the hundreds of thousands. Experts estimate that grizzlies can consume around 40,000 moths per day and close to one million per month. For grizzlies, finding one of these sites is like finding several meals. The moths provide a crucial fat source for the grizzlies, especially since their other primary staple food, the whitebark pine nut, is disappearing. If one grizzly eats one million moths per month, this will account for 47% of that bear's annual caloric budget.

The benefits of this relationship are evident for the grizzlies. The bears get access to food high in fat, but they also are eating at high elevations. This may be just as important because if bears are high on slopes, it means that they are not down in valleys along roadsides or near residential areas where they could get into trouble. Eating this high keeps the bears away from potential conflicts with people. How does this relationship impact moth populations?

Even though moths are being eaten in massive amounts, they are not at risk of extinction because of their rapid reproductive rate. People view the army cutworm moth as an agricultural and garden pest because of the insect's enormous appetite for leaves, buds, and stems. They have been known to defoliate entire gardens and fields in a matter of days. Moths have had problems with public relations for a long time. Maybe the fact that they could help grizzly bears is just what the moths need to redeem their name.

Because these moths aggregate on high slopes, they are rare for the average tourist to observe. However, there's another flying creature in Yellowstone that is not so hard to see or hear. In fact, it would be rare not to see one.

Chapter 12

Wolves of the Sky

$$-\,.\,\overline{-}\,.\,\overline{-}\,.\,\overline{-}\,.\,\overline{-}$$

Luck is seldom as haphazard as it may seem. It means being at the right place at the right time, and most of all, it means being prepared to take advantage of opportunities.

-Bernd Heinrich,
Mind of the Raven

THE AMERICAN ULTRARUNNING ASSOCIATION HALL-of-Fame inducted Berndt Heinrich in 2007. Throughout the 1980s, Heinrich won some ultramarathons, which are very long-distance running events. In 1983, Heinrich ran 156 miles over a span of twenty-four hours on a track in Maine, an American record. Even with all his running accomplishments, Heinrich is more widely known as one of the most accomplished scientists and naturalists with a wide range of expertise. The two are not mutually exclusive. Heinrich's natural curiosity coupled with his ability to apply sound theory allowed him to succeed in running and science.

Heinrich was born in Germany in 1940. Both of his parents were biologists. As the war was approaching an end, his family moved to the forest of northern Germany to escape the invading Soviets. While in the woods, Heinrich and his sister trapped mice and found carcasses for food. They also had to forage for plants to eat. In 1951, the family moved to Maine, where Heinrich attended a boarding school. Heinrich went on to complete his Ph.D. in Zoology from UCLA, and then became a professor at the University of California-Berkeley. Most of his research centered around the behavior and comparative physiology of social insects. Heinrich is considered an expert on temperature regulation of moths, bumblebees, and honeybees. He wrote the book on the mechanisms of this regulation called *Bumblebee Economics*. In 1980, Heinrich took a job at the University of Vermont. Living in the woods in western Maine, Heinrich designed scientific studies based on his observations, of which he seems to have an endless supply. Many of these studies were designed while he was out running in the woods. Some revolve around ravens. Like Heinrich, we too should step back and let curiosity guide us. If not, we could be missing out on small wonders. Heinrich has peered into the world of common animals like ravens and found many bizarre and extraordinary interactions. In fact, Heinrich has published many interesting papers about the social behavior of ravens.

Ravens, like other members of the corvid family, show a high level of intelligence. They show evidence of planning by their ability to hoard food. One recent study showed that ravens could plan for events other than caching food. Researchers found that ravens could use tools to get food surprises and could barter for tools or food if need be. In these experiments, ravens outperformed four-year-old children.

In Yellowstone, ravens have been observed taking part in what we might call playful behavior. One winter, our group watched ravens on the back of a snowmobile. They opened the back flap, which was held together with Velcro and then pulled out two Ziploc bags of trail mix. They opened the bags and ate the snacks. We have observed similar behavior in the Old Faithful parking lot during the busy summer season. One afternoon, we counted thirty ravens in the bed of a pick-up truck. They had opened food bags and coolers, and were enjoying a great feast. The owners of the truck were going to be in for quite the surprise when they returned from the geyser.

More so than careless human and unattended snacks, the return of wolves to Yellowstone has benefited ravens. When wolves are feeding at a carcass, ravens are always there. In fact, ravens arrive at the carcass almost instantly, usually before the rest of the wolf pack comes. This behavior makes researchers wonder if there is a unique relationship between wolves and ravens in Yellowstone. Ravens possibly monitor wolf pack activities by following them directly, following their tracks, or by responding to vocalizations. Maybe they are guilty of all three.

Typically, ravens are present in the majority of wolf bouts with elk but tend to be absent around coyote and elk conflicts. This would seem to provide good evidence of a relationship between these two species. One study found that ravens spent more time with wolves when the wolves were chasing prey than when wolves were just traveling. Ravens hardly spent any time hanging around wolves when the wolves were bedded down resting. The birds seem to know when food is coming.

Unanswered Questions 12.1
1. Why do wolves tolerate ravens at a carcass?
2. Can ravens gather information from wolves regarding carcass location?
3. Do ravens show wolves where to find unhealthy elk?
4. Is it possible that ravens have developed behavioral mechanisms for detecting and locating large carcasses?

In winter, ungulate carcasses represent an unpredictable food source for ravens, in both space and time. Therefore, it benefits these birds to associate with wolves. Kleptoparasitism is the process by which species like scavengers steal food. It happens when there is a predator/scavenger interaction. Tagging along with a predator reduces the time it takes for the raven to find food, lowers the risk factors, and lowers the energy expenditure. By following wolves, ravens can discover bison and elk buffets. They could undoubtedly find these carcasses using other strategies like flying over the land and seeing the food or following other ravens. However, nagging wolves seems to be the most productive.

Prior to the reintroduction of wolves in 1995, scavengers had to rely on harsh winters to kill elk and bison. With wolves, who are very efficient predators, more elk and bison carcasses are available throughout the year although very few bison carcasses are a direct result of wolves killing them. Because wolves cannot or do not consume all of every carcass, scavengers usually have an opportunity to fill their bellies. Researchers studied various factors that determine how much of a carcass wolves will consume. Pack size seems to be a significant predictor. Larger packs eat more of a carcass, thus leaving less for scavengers. As expected, an increase in the mass of the prey animal decreased the percent consumption by wolves. The wolves just became full and satisfied before they were able to devour the entire carcass. Carcasses that were closer to roads also tended to be least consumed by wolves, presumably because of their uneasiness around humans. Ravens take advantage of all of these sites by arriving immediately and eating selectively.

While researchers have yet to show that ravens and wolves help each other hunt and kill prey, there's substantial evidence of this mutualistic behavior in two different predators.

Chapter 13

Diggers and Chasers

‒ . ‒ . . ‒ . ‒

When you're down and troubled and you need a helping hand and
nothing, whoa, nothing is going right...All you got to do is call and
I'll be there... You've got a friend.

-James Taylor

TRUFFLEHUNTER IS AN OLD WORLD NARNIAN IN C.S.
Lewis's book series *The Chronicles of Narnia*. He makes his first
appearance in the book *Prince Caspian*, in which an evil group
of warriors is ruling the land of Narnia. These men are determined to drive out all of the old world Narnians, including the
talking beasts. The rightful king of Narnia, Caspian, flees the
castle after being warned about the plot to have him killed. As
he is riding away on his horse, Caspian hits his head on a low
tree branch and is knocked unconscious. Trufflehunter finds
Caspian and tends his wounds. When Caspian regains con-
sciousness, he is surprised to see that Trufflehunter is a talking
badger. Throughout the story, Trufflehunter fights at Caspian's side and shows great wisdom as he offers advice. All of
the old Narnians look forward to the return of Aslan the lion,
who they hope will return to save and restore Narnia. Trufflehunter never loses faith. "I am a beast, and I am a Badger

what's more," he says. "We don't change. We hold on." He goes on to say, "Have patience, like us beasts. The help will come."

Like Trufflehunter, wild badgers are known for their relentless behavior and determination. The American badger, *Taxidea taxus*, is no different. Badgers belong to the same family as otters, weasels, and wolverines. Mustelids are a species-rich family that first appeared fifteen million years ago. The American version packs a lot of energy into its twenty-pound frame. They are stocky with mighty legs. At the ends of these legs are two-inch claws that act as shovels as they dig. The most identifiable characteristic is the badger's triangular face with dark brown cheek markings and a white stripe that runs from the base of the head to the nose. They appear to have been marked with war paint.

Badgers that we have observed in Yellowstone have had one thing in common: they appeared to be on a mission, just as one looks when going into battle. During one trip, we had been told by some friends that a family of badgers had a den and were quite easy to see just off a popular trail. Fortunately for us, we were planning on hiking this trail. We were excited about the possibility. It only took several minutes for me to get distracted looking for salamander eggs near a pond right off the trail. As I bent over to search along the edge of the water, one of our participants yelled, "There's a badger! Look, over there!" As the rest of us turned in the direction, we saw it. The badger was moving fast in a zig-zagging motion. She was definitely on a mission as she followed the alarm signals of the nearby ground squirrels. We watched her for several minutes before she finally disappeared in the sage.

Several years later, we had another opportunity to watch a badger successfully hunt. We left Cooke City, MT one afternoon to travel west back into the Lamar Valley when we saw one run onto the road, move in several circles, and then sprint into the sage. As we approached, all we could see (or get a picture of) was badger bum. What we heard, though, told us everything we needed to know. Ground squirrels were calling from everywhere, but one, in particular, seemed to be in high distress. After several failed pounces, we heard an awful squeal right before the badger came up with a mouthful of a squirrel. We were filled with mixed emotions as we thought about what we had just witnessed. There is a rush of adrenaline when you observe a wild predator hunting. Though, there's a part of you that feels sorry for the prey.

In and around Yellowstone, Uinta ground squirrels, *Urocitellus armatus*, serve as a prey buffet for predators like badgers. These ground squirrels are small, only measuring twelve inches in length, but are plentiful in sage and grass flats. They live in colonies and are only active for a few months each year. Adult ground squirrels head into their burrows at the end of July and do not emerge from hibernation until mid-March. It is their sociality (or lack thereof) that they rely on most. They live in dense aggregations but seem to not be very family-oriented. Males are promiscuous, females do not care for their young once the young are above ground, and juveniles do not tolerate one another. However, because they do live closely together, the sounds that they use in response to threats do help others. Ground squirrels use many different types of sounds to communicate.

Donna Mae Balph was a graduate student at Utah State University in the early 1960s. For her thesis, she researched sound communication in the Uinta ground squirrels. Balph spent countless hours in the field observing these squirrels. She parked her truck at a field station near Logan, Utah and used it as a blind as she recorded all sounds that these squirrels made. Balph also recorded what the callers were doing and how other squirrels reacted. This research is a perfect example of field researchers showing great patience as they work to find answers to nature's questions. Balph found her answers. She showed that these squirrels produce six distinct sounds with different meanings: *chirps, churrs, squeals, squawks, teeth-chatters*, and *growls*. *Chirps* are used by males during breeding seasons to call females, but also outside of breeding seasons to alert other males to keep a healthy distance. *Chirping* in females usually accompanies aggressive behaviors, especially when they are pregnant. The *churr* call is only used by females to warn other females not to come close. Subordinate squirrels use the *squeal* when attacked by the more established squirrels. *Growls* are typically the result of threats from other squirrels. Interestingly, Balph found that squirrels used *chirps* in response to airborne predators, such as red-tailed hawks. For ground predators, like badgers, the squirrels used *churrs* as the standard warning sound. Usually, only one to two squirrels called, but they called continuously until the threat passed. These *churrs* function to warn other squirrels, but not instantly. Uinta ground squirrels are either skeptical of other squirrels or just paranoid, because when they hear an alarm call, they do not immediately run to their safe underground space. Most of the time, they stand up and look for themselves. This pause is what cost the squirrel his life the afternoon we observed the badger hunt.

The third time we observed a badger in YNP, he was not alone. We stopped at a pullout near Blacktail Ponds along the northern section. Our objective was to get out, stretch our legs, and talk about what we had experienced during that particular trip. As often happens at the roadside pullouts, participants get distracted. This time, a sprinting coyote drew the attention of several students in our group. We stopped what we were doing to get out the scope and binoculars. As we watched, we noticed that the coyote would often pause and turn his head while staring at the ground. He would then resume his run. At one of his stops, a figure emerged from behind. We instantly saw that the new animal was a badger, but why would a badger be hanging out this close to a coyote? As we watched we noticed that these two different species were content. They both seemed interested in the ground squirrels running around. Why, though, would they be tolerating each other's presence? Could they be cooperating?

It is not unusual for two predators to help each other. However, it would seem counterintuitive at first glance for a badger and a coyote to cooperatively hunt because their prey items overlap. They both love ground squirrels. Competition should be the result.

Steve Minta, a biologist with the University of California Davis, published a paper based on 214 badger/coyote interactions that he observed. Of these interactions, 90% of them took place between a single coyote and a single badger, 9% were between one badger and two coyotes, and only 1% involved one badger and three coyotes. These data tell us something important. Cooperative hunts work best when there are only two individuals. There may not be enough food to go around for four animals. Minta's observations all shared similarities. One, the badgers were good at digging into the squirrel burrows. Two, the coyotes did a great job chasing the squirrels.

According to Minta, badgers and coyotes excelled in a type of hunting behavior that the other lacked. The badgers would dig to find the squirrels. Sometimes the badger would catch its prey, but often the squirrels would pop above ground and run. When this happened, the nearby coyote would take off after the squirrel. Advantage coyote. On the other hand, the coyotes cannot catch every squirrel they chase. Once a squirrel dove into an underground burrow the chase would end. A rodent playing hide-and-seek would then give the badger the chance to dig and find the squirrel. Advantage badger. This game can be played over and over until the two predators satisfy their stomachs.

Trufflehunter may have been right. Be patient, and help may come, even if it is in the form of a fellow predator.

Part Four:
Unconventional
Adaptations

This American pronghorn is built for speed.

Chapter 14

Natural Selection Primer

— — . — . — . — . —

Evolution thus is merely contingent on certain processes articulated by Darwin: variation and selection.

- Ernst Mayr

ORGANISMS IN YELLOWSTONE HAVE STRUCTURES AND behaviors that enable them to persist and reproduce. Some of these make perfect sense to us. Some cause us to pause and question. The chapters in this part contain stories about adaptations. If we are going to discuss evolution and adaptation, we must have another conversation about Charles Darwin. Let's look at his theory before we look at specific examples.

Darwin proposed a mechanism for evolution called natural selection. It is essential to understand what natural selection is and what it is not to know how this process forms the foundation of the great diversity of organisms. The following shows the five main points of natural selection:

1) Individuals within a species are variable.

2) Some of these variations are passed on to offspring.

3) In every generation, more offspring are produced than can survive.

4) Survival and reproduction are not random. The individuals that survive and go on to reproduce, or who reproduce the most, are those with the most favorable variations. They are naturally selected.

5) Species multiplication– As species move through time, in a manner described by the previous four points, species split, and new ones form. 99% of all species that have ever lived are extinct.

The following model may help with understandings Darwin's thoughts:

Observation 1: Organisms have great potential fertility, which permits exponential growth of populations.

Observation 2: Natural populations typically do not increase exponentially, but remain relatively constant in size.

Observation 3: Natural resources are limited.

- **Inference 1**: A struggle for existence occurs among organisms within populations because resources are limited.

Observation 4: Variation occurs among organisms within populations.

Observation 5: Variation is heritable.

- **Inference 2**: Varying organisms show differential survival and reproduction, favoring advantageous traits.
- **Inference 3**: Natural selection, acting over many generations, gradually produces new species.

Natural selection leads to adaptations of species over time. This process, however, does not involve a species trying, wanting, or needing a particular adjustment. Populations evolve. Individuals do not. Natural selection results from genetic variation in a population (see Observations 4 and 5 above). This genetic variation is generated by random mutations, which is independent of what an individual within a population needs.

In this section, we will look at a variety of adaptations across different species. Some of the adaptations we will discuss show how species survive and thrive in their natural ecosystems. Some even show how species flourish in foreign ecosystems.

Chapter 15

Guilty and Never Proven
Innocent

-.-.-.-.-.-

We must make no mistake: we are seeing one of the great historical convulsions in the world's fauna and flora. We might say, with Professor Challenger, standing on Conan Doyle's "Lost World", with his black beard jutting out: "We have been privileged to be present at one of the typical decisive battles of history—the battles which have determined the fate of the world." But how will it be decisive? Will it be a Lost World? These are the questions that ecologists ought to try to answer.

-Charles Elton,
The Ecology of Invasions by Animals and Plants

GUSTAVUS CHEYNEY DOANE WAS A CAPTAIN IN THE U.S. Army. As an explorer, he was a vital member of both the 1870 Washburn Expedition to Yellowstone and the 1871 Hayden Geological Survey. The stories, testimonies, and pictures from these explorations helped convince Congress that this land needed protecting. Doane also helped spread the word to recreational fishermen that the land was a haven and a dream because of the high population and diversity of fish in the park. He wrote that Yellowstone's trout numbers were "perfectly fabulous" and that with only grasshoppers as bait, "the most awkward angler can fill a champagne basket in an hour or two."

What Doane didn't know at the time was that 40% of the waters in the area were devoid of fish. Once the U.S. established the land as a park in 1872, some early park superintendents asked the U.S. Fish Commission to stock all waters within and around Yellowstone with fish to supplement recreational fishing. They wanted visitors to be satisfied. Part of this stocking effort in the late 1800s included the addition of lake trout. The commission was blind to the impact this would have on the native species. The native cutthroat trout were not prepared to deal with the much larger lake trout. One lake trout could eat as many as ninety cutthroats per year. The aquatic ecosystem of Yellowstone found itself in the middle of a crisis because of the cutthroat's importance.

Around forty species depend on the cutthroat trout as an essential part of their diet, including many species of birds, bears, coyotes, and otters. Lake trout do not provide the same food source. Cutthroats prefer to live and spawn in shallow water which makes it easier for the predators to hunt them. The lake trout, on the other hand, like to stay in deeper water, and they spawn at different times than that cutthroat. Since the cutthroats are such a central food source and a nutrient link to the rest of the environment, their continued decline and possible extinction could change the ecosystem drastically. Also, fishing for cutthroat has supported a $36 million annual sports fishery, making it an essential part of the economy. The blame for the cutthroat disaster, however, does not rest solely on the lake trout. There is another invasive to blame for the cutthroat's demise.

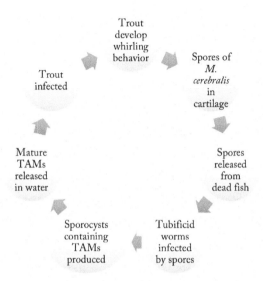

FIG 15.1. *M. Cerebralis* **life cycle**

In 1893, just twenty-three years after Doane's first trip to Yellowstone, small parasitic organisms called myxosporea were first detected. This animal was named *Myxobolus cerebralis* in 1903 because scientists thought it infected the brain. However, it is a parasite of skeletal tissue. *M. cerebralis* does not resemble a typical animal. For one, it is microscopic, just 150 micrometers long in its mature form. It also has two life cycles in which it causes a condition called whirling disease. How it operates in an ecosystem is similar to something you would expect to see in a science fiction film—both fascinating and disastrous.

This particular parasite has an obligate host, a type of sludge worm called *Tubifex tubifex*, that lives in sediments of lakes and rivers. During the myxosporean stage of their life cycle, sludge worms ingest the spores that measure only ten micrometers in diameter. These myxospores get into the worm and attach to the lining of the worm's gut, where they start to multiply. Between sixty to ninety days after the initial infection, some of the spores are released by the worm's anus into the water column.

The parasite then enters another part of the life cycle, the triactinomyxon (TAM) spore. These spores are different. The TAM comes equipped with a long central style, measuring around 150 micrometers attached to three tails. It travels through the water and can infect the cutthroat by first attaching to the outer epithelium layer of tissue. The parasite eventually makes its way into the nervous system of the fish and then into the cartilage. The infection causes tail deformities and also a whirling behavior in the fish, where the fish begins to chase its tail. More importantly, it also causes death. The parasite's life comes full circle when the myxospore is created in the fish and released back into the water after the fish either is eaten or decomposes.

Researchers first recorded *M. cerebralis* in the U.S. in 1956 in Pennsylvania. Supposedly, a trout imported from Europe introduced it. Scientists first noticed it in the pristine waters of Yellowstone Lake in 1998. As with the lake trout, *M. cerebralis* threatens the integrity of this naturally functioning ecosystem by causing severe declines in wild trout populations.

It also has a negative economic impact by decreasing the opportunities for recreational fishing. Park managers have estimated that this parasite has spread to around 20% of the cutthroat population, the most widespread outbreaks occurring in the Pelican Creek tributary and the Yellowstone River section just downstream of the lake outlet. Managers are not sure what else to do besides encourage anglers and boaters to clean mud and vegetation from all equipment before moving from one spot to another to decrease the chance of contamination.

Management decisions are tough, especially with non-native, exotic parasites. What makes non-native, or in this case, invasive species so challenging to manage is the fact that their biology may not be entirely understood or even easily studied. It is usually impossible to guess whether non-native species will become established in a foreign ecosystem, and even if they do, we don't know how they are going to impact native species. Decisions on how to manage are also challenging when we use the words "non-native" and "invasive" to mean the same thing. To properly handle species, we need to make sure we are using accurate terminology.

The U.S. Department of Agriculture defines an invasive species as "plants, animals, or pathogens that are non-native (or alien) to the ecosystem under consideration, *and* whose introduction causes or is likely to cause harm." This may not be an adequate definition. The "and" in the definition seems to be key.

Unanswered Questions 15.1
1. What are the qualifications for calling a species "native" or "non-native"?
2. What should be done with non-native species that do not cause harm to an ecosystem?
3. How should we label native species that cause harm?
4. How do we decide if a species is causing harm?

Terminology is important because land and wildlife managers make decisions to allocate resources based on these terms. For a species like *M. cerebralis*, the terminology seems to be straightforward. For other species that carry the labels of "invasive" and "non-native," the answers to these questions are blurry.

Mountain goats, *Oreamnos americanus*, live in alpine habitats of the Rocky Mountains, including parts of the Greater Yellowstone Ecosystem. Historically, they roamed along the western coast from Alaska to northern Washington and in the Rocky Mountains from northern Canada to northern Montana. Specific state agencies introduced populations successfully into other parts of the Rocky Mountains. In the Absaroka Range, twenty-three goats were released between 1956-1958 by the Montana Fish and Game Department. They wanted to provide recreational hunting opportunities for residents and visitors. These goats came from native herds in southwest Montana. Between 1942-1956, managers released thirty-nine goats in the eastern Beartooth Mountains. Yellowstone officials estimate the current population of goats to be around 200. They have adapted quite well and established themselves.

Mountain goats cause a problem, though. The problem is not necessarily with the ecosystem, but with wildlife managers. The goats leave managers and park service employees confused on how to label them. For example, Yellowstone has signs that indicate these goats are non-native. However, since they evolved along the western coastal ranges and in some parts of the Rocky Mountains, this labeling seems short-sighted. Another confusing part is that in some definitions, including the one above by the U.S. Department of Agriculture, the term "non-native" always implies invasive.

Ecologists have wrestled with this problem. They often struggle over whether they should ever introduce a non-native species to try to control another non-native species. This particular issue is directly related to another confusing species, a plant all too familiar to those living in the southeastern U.S.

The Centennial Exposition of 1876, held in Philadelphia, celebrated the 100th anniversary of the signing of the Declaration of Independence. From May through October, almost ten million people were exposed to 30,000 exhibits from all over the world. Plant exhibitions were widely popular, and among those was a delegation from Japan that had brought a plant with large leaves and fragrant blooms called *Pueraria labata*, commonly known as kudzu. American gardeners were instantly attracted. No one knows how many times the plant exchanged hands during this fair, but we do know that seventeen years later at another world fair in Chicago two nursery operators would become huge fans.

During the 1920s, these operators discovered that livestock would eat kudzu, so they began selling it all over the U.S. Kudzu was even used by the U.S. Soil Conservation Service for erosion control in the 1930s. In the 1940s, farmers were paid eight dollars per acre to plant kudzu fields. Unfortunately, we know how this story ends. People, especially those that live in the southeast, see kudzu everywhere. It grows well and has been very successful at establishing itself.

In 2009, another Asian import, *Megacopta criteria*, the kudzu bug, was observed in Georgia. This bug spread throughout the southeast and established in the same areas as kudzu. These insects have an appetite for kudzu, but they also like to eat soybeans. In a case such as this, would it be appropriate to raise these bugs in a laboratory just to release them in specific areas with the hope that they will rid us of the kudzu problem? Should we use non-native and potentially invasive species to control another exotic species?

Where does that leave us with labeling species and making informed management decisions? Kudzu has been here since right after 1876. It has been successful at adapting and making itself part of the native ecosystem. It does not look as if we are ever going to rid the ecosystem of it. We can agree that it is non-native. We can also agree that it is invasive, at least to a certain degree. We should even agree that, with species such as this, we could be smarter about how we allocate resources. If calling kudzu native makes us feel like we do not have to try to get rid of it altogether, maybe that is what we should do.

For mountain goats, we have already established the fact that it is not fair to call them non-native. Research shows that they are not invasive. Maybe we should accept that they are native and a current functional part of Yellowstone's ecosystem.

Researchers agree that *M. cerebralis* is both non-native and invasive. This parasite is disrupting native species like the cutthroat. Since it has not taken entirely over aquatic ecosystems like Yellowstone Lake and its tributaries, maybe the *M. cerebralis* story will have a different ending than kudzu. Complete eradication could be possible. Perhaps, the future waters of Yellowstone will be naturally functioning ecosystems, and the trout will live up to being "perfectly fabulous," just as Captain Doane described them in 1870.

Even within naturally functioning ecosystems, sometimes we come across animals with outrageous body structures that make us wonder how they survive year after year. Some just don't seem to make sense. We'll look at some of these structures next.

Chapter 16

Extreme Weapons

-.-.-.-.-.-

As weapons get bigger they select for increasingly elaborate deterrence, and deterrence, in turn, selects for bigger and bigger weapons. Arms races and deterrence push each other forward, escalating in an evolutionary spiral.

-Doug Emlen,
Animal Weapons

IMAGINE SITTING ON THE SOFA READING A BOOK, AND suddenly you see something small and gray moving across the floor. Once you get over the shock of seeing a mouse in your house, you begin to devise a plan to trap it. Now, imagine if the mouse you saw had two horns protruding from its forehead. Up until about six million years ago, there was an odd family of rodents, the Mylagaulidae, that did have horns. In fact, they are the only rodents known to have ever had horns. Mylagaulid fossils have been found in almost all the North American faunas, and are thought to have developed from a family that includes the mountain beaver. Researchers have tried to determine why these rodents had horns and why no rodent species living today have horns. There must be possible motives for the evolution of horned rodents and reasons for their extinction. Fortunately, scientists are not entirely clueless.

The horns could have been the direct result of outside environmental pressures to survive (natural selection). Another possibility is that the horns could have initially increased the success of mating for the males (sexual selection). Also, both natural and sexual selection could have been the reason. Let's weigh the evidence for each type.

If horns were exclusively the result of environmental pressures (natural selection), the rodents should have exhibited several specific behaviors. For example, horns could have helped them survive by digging underground tunnels to escape the threat of predators. While most rodents today use their claws and teeth to help with digging, horns may have made these rodents more efficient burrowers. These horned rodents had characteristics such as large neck muscles and thickened nasal bones to indicate that they did use their heads for digging, and some research has shown that the horns were thick and flat. Other research shows that the skulls of these rodents were low and broad, characteristics not ideal for head-lift digging. This indicates that the horns may have evolved for some other purpose.

Another behavior that would support the idea that the horns were a result of environmental pressures would be that these rodents used the horns in defending against predators. The horned rodents probably became extinct because of competition from species of the gopher family. It was this competition along with the changing landscape of the period in which they lived that eventually drove these rodents to live underground. The horns, which were broad enough at the base to cover the neck and eyes, may have evolved as mechanisms to help the rodents fend off predators. Horns such as these are present in the Bovidae family, which includes sheep, cattle, antelope, and bison. Competition between species led the horns of these animals to be shaped differently because of various fighting techniques. While we can make arguments for horn development due to environmental pressure, it is also possible that the horns evolved earlier because of sexual selective pressure, increasing successful mating.

If the horns were sexually dimorphic (found in males, but not females), male-male combat would have been a typical behavior in these types of rodents. The males may have used these horns to fight off rival males who were interested in stealing mates. Horn size in sheep, antelope, cattle, and bison plays a significant role in sexual interactions; the larger the horns are in males, the more successful they are at mating. Horns may have served the same purpose in these rodents. The males with the most massive horns would have had an advantage during battles, and so they would have won the right to mate with the more fertile females. The males with the smallest horns, or none at all, would have had a lesser chance to mate; therefore, they would not have been able to pass their genes to the next generation.

Another behavior supporting sexual selection would be the use of the horns for guarding females after mating. Paternity is extremely important to males of most species, who instinctively want their genetic traits to continue. The horns may have helped the males ensure paternity by allowing them to guard the females before and after copulation. One approach might have been to defensively guard the entrance of the tunnels so that rival males could not enter and copulate with the female. For example, male golden hamsters sleep between the opening of the burrow and the female to fend off any male competition. When they do decide to copulate with the female, they do so frequently to increase their chances of fathering the offspring. Another example is that of the male purple martin, who also fends off rival males until he ensures paternity. Once the female begins to incubate the eggs, he will allow other males into the nest. He then will show promiscuous behavior by leaving to copulate with unattended females. A male horned rodent could have done the same— ensured paternity with his mate and then traveled to other underground tunnels to mate with other females and father their offspring as well. Pre- or post-copulatory guarding would have allowed a male the security of protecting his sperm and fathering multiple offspring.

Finally, if horns were the result of sexual selection, these male rodents would have used the horns as a form of sexual display to attract females as potential mates. In many species, males tend to be larger than females for this very reason. An example of such sexual display happens in male sea lions, which flaunt a massive mane, grow up to three times larger than the female sea lions, and can attract many females at one time to become part of their harem. Male peacocks, which fan their bright tail feathers in hopes of inviting a suitable mating partner, are another example. Similarly, males of the Bovidae family have more success mating if they possess large horns.

Males of these all species use their appearance to intimidate rival males as well as attract the most selective females. Females want their offspring to be fit and healthy; therefore, they try to choose the best-looking males as mates. The horns of these rodents could have developed because they were traits females found desirable and consequently wanted their offspring to possess. However, it is hard to say whether the horns developed just as a result of sexual selection.

What we do know is that research shows the rodents developed horns for a definite purpose, whether as a result of natural selection or sexual selection. Most likely, the horns increased both the survival rate and reproductive success of this family. The horns probably also began an evolutionary race between the sexes.

The same evidence for the evolution of rodent horns applies to some of the animals we see in Yellowstone. For example, moose, elk, and bighorn sheep all show sexual dimorphism when it comes to antler and horn development. The males possess the extreme weapons in these species. But, why?

In most animals, the drive to breed and produce offspring is strong. However, most males live their whole lives without having the chance to reproduce. Events leading up to mating can be hazardous and costly to an individual. Some males have evolved elaborate structures, or weapons, as a result. The structures do help males in both combative situations and with attracting females, but ironically, the structures themselves come with certain costs. In some cases, the structures may not always be used as weapons.

In his book, *Animal Weapons: The Evolution of Battle*, Douglas Emlen notes that the most successful animal weapons almost never get used because there is no need. A bighorn ram or a bull elk, for example, often protect their harem by showing opponents their big antler racks, which deter others from fighting.

Animals have structures that come in a variety of shapes and sizes and often are suited to perform a specific function. Some animals seem to take this to the extreme. Life is organized at all levels. Animals are multicellular organisms that have specialized cells grouped into tissues. Combinations of tissues make up units called organs, and groups of organs that work together are called organ systems. The complementary relationship between anatomy, or structure, and physiology, or function, is seen at each level. Here are a few examples of how specific structures that make up an animal's body plan are related to a specific function:

- Mule deer have ears that are very large to enhance their ability to hear.
- Northern flickers have a slightly curved bill that makes it easy for them to dig for ants and beetles.
- Wolves have a thick undercoat that is oily and waterproof which provides excellent insulation against cold weather.
- Pronghorn have a large windpipe, heart, and lungs with an extremely light bone structure which make it the fastest land mammal in the western hemisphere.

- Bison have large shoulder muscles that aid them in "plowing" snow to get to the vegetation.
- Ravens have a beak shaped like a knife, which they use for tearing and carving.

Natural selection is the underlying factor in the "structure compliments function" concept. Darwin, though, even observed animals that seem to have elaborate structures when he wrote the following:

"How low in the scale of nature this law of battle descends, I know not; male alligators have been described as fighting, bellowing, and whirling round, like Indians in a war-dance, for the possession of the females; male salmons have been seen fighting all day long; male stag-beetles often bear wounds from the huge mandibles of other males. The war is, perhaps, severest between the males of polygamous animals, and these seem oftenest provided with special weapons."

All of these extreme structures require an energy investment since cells and tissues need energy for growth and maintenance. Even though the body plan of an animal is the result of millions of years of evolution, physical requirements limit what natural selection can do. For example, elephants do not fly because an animal that large, even if it had wings, could not generate enough lift to take off and fly. Also, there are only certain ways an aquatic organism can be shaped to be a fast swimmer. It is helpful to understand bioenergetics, the flow of energy through an animal, to understand animal structures.

Animals are heterotrophs and must obtain their chemical energy in food, which contains organic molecules synthesized by other organisms. After body cells absorb the food molecules, most of the food is used to generate ATP by cellular respiration and fermentation. The chemical energy of ATP powers cellular work and enables cells, tissues, organs, and organ systems to perform many functions that keep an animal alive. The amount of energy an animal uses in a unit of time is called its metabolic rate. This metabolic rate can be measured by monitoring an animal's heat loss or by determining the amount of oxygen consumed or carbon dioxide produced.

There are two bioenergetic strategies used by animals. Birds and mammals are mainly endothermic, which means they maintain their body temperature within a narrow range, with heat generated by metabolism. Most fishes, amphibians, reptiles, and invertebrates are ectothermic, meaning they gain their heat mostly from external sources. Ectotherms require much less energy than is needed by endotherms because of the energy cost of heating or cooling an endothermic body.

One of biology's most intriguing and mostly unanswered questions has to do with the relationship between body plans and metabolic rate. Every animal has a range of metabolic rates. Minimal rates power the essential functions that support life, such as cell maintenance, breathing, and heartbeat. For most animals, the majority of food is devoted to the production of ATP, and relatively little goes toward growth. However, for an animal with an extreme structure, there is an enormous investment towards the growth and maintenance of that structure.

Researchers want to know how animals cope with the risks of having large, elaborate structures. In a species of dung beetle, researchers showed that as the insect allocates more resources to building an elaborate horn, it allocates fewer resources to the growth of testes. This trade-off would seem counterproductive. The horns of rodents could very well have developed with similar fitness trade-offs. The male rodents did have small eyes, a trait the horns could have caused, and poor eyesight. Both of these could have led to their extinction for several reasons. The horned rodents may not have been able to see, and therefore avoid, oncoming predators. In and around Yellowstone, moose spend up to 50% of their food energy just growing antlers. Their skeletons lose calcium and phosphorus to the building of these structures. This leaves their bones brittle and weak. One would think that natural selection would have "weeded" out these animals that invest heavily in massive structures.

Obviously, the benefits of having these weapons outweigh the costs. The answer to 'Why?' may simply be deterrence. Maybe animals like moose, elk, and bighorn rams have large weapons so that they do not have to fight. Evolution favors elaborate structures in these specific animals. As we will soon find out, the pressures of evolution do not only influence body structures. Sometimes, these pressures play a role in how animals construct their homes.

Chapter 17

Mud nests

−.−.−.−.−.−

There's no place like home.

-Dorothy Gale

BIRDS BUILD THEIR HOMES IN VARIOUS PLACES. FOR some birds, tree branches or cavities make a suitable location. For others, building on the ground is perfectly suitable. One species prefers to build a nest out of mud.

Searching along the banks of a river for mud may sound like a dirty job. However, if you are a cliff swallow, *Petrochelidon pyrrhonota*, it is simply a way of life. Cliff swallows find mud and gather it in their bills to use as the primary nest building material. The swallows bring the mud pellets back to the side of a cliff, cave, or even a man-made structure to construct a conical, gourd-shaped nest. In Yellowstone, they really like outhouses. This strange type of building behavior requires us to ask some questions. For example, what is the point of collecting mud and other debris to construct an odd-looking nest? Why do cliff swallows prefer to build these types of nests in colonies? To answer some of these it is important to look at the reasons for having nests in the first place.

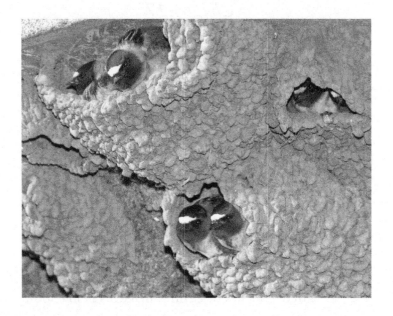

FIG 17.1. **Cliff swallows build their nests in colonies.**

There is a tremendous amount of variation in nest design among animal groups. Some mammals dig burrows, fish construct craters, and termites build mounds. Even though the design may be different, nests serve as a place where animals lay eggs and raise their young. The types of mud nests that cliff swallows build must be associated with benefits and costs.

Unanswered Questions 17.1
1. Why would cliff swallows go through the trouble of building gourd-shaped nests attached to the side of a building near other nests?
2. What roles do natural and sexual selection play in nest building?

Nests can impact the fitness of individual birds. Typically, ecologists define fitness as how successful individuals are in passing their genes to the next generation. The higher the fitness of an individual, the higher the chances of surviving and reproducing. Many environmental factors influence the fitness levels of individuals. This is especially true of cliff swallow behavior. First, the location and design of nests both contribute to predator avoidance. Also, building nests in a colony can increase social interactions which, in turn, can increase the chances of survival. These strategies show that natural selection exerts strong selective pressures on the design and placement of nests, but natural selection does not explain everything.

In addition to being influenced by natural selection, nest design may also be the result of sexual selection. More specifically, the pressures from sexual selection can result in what is called extended phenotypic signals. Phenotype refers to an organism's physical and observable characteristics. This can include an animal's appearance, how large or small it is, how it develops, how it behaves, or even the results of its behavior— such as the construction of a nest. In one of his landmark books, Richard Dawkins took this a step further when he defined the extended phenotype as "an animal artifact, like any other phenotypic product whose variation is influenced by a gene."

Some species of birds have individuals who signal their quality, or how much they are worth, through physical signals like bright plumage. Other individual birds indicate quality through behavioral signals like dancing. According to scientists, nest building is just like bright plumage or fancy dancing. For example, Bowerbirds build structures whose sole purpose is to attract a mate. If nest-building behavior and nest design is an extended phenotype in cliff swallows that plays a role in sexual selection, then there must be some costs associated with the builder. One of those obstacles may be the presence of external parasites, referred to as ectoparasitism.

Cliff swallows are highly social birds. They feed, preen, gather mud, and participate in most activities socially. As we have mentioned, they also nest in colonies. It is this sociality that may explain why bloodthirsty swallow bugs (*Oeciacus vicarious*) and fleas (*Ceratophyllus celcus*) parasitize the birds. Swallow bugs are found almost exclusively on cliff swallows and can remain permanently in nests, except for a period of dispersal in the spring in which they hitch a ride at the base of the swallows' feathers. Swallow bugs lower the body mass and survivorship of chicks by 50% in large colonies, but not in small colonies. Thus, parasitism is a severe cost of nesting close. The presence of parasites probably contributes to the selection of nests or the need to build new nests.

One particular study showed that colony sites vary in their suitability. The researchers concluded that colony sites that had the highest reproductive success relative to others tended to be re-used the following year, even by new immigrants. Birds select nesting sites that have the least concentration of parasites, and thus increase the chances of offspring survival. Even though females probably do most of the nest site selecting, single males have been observed selecting and also building a new nest to attract a mate.

Swallows select nesting sites and then build these mud nests with two things in mind: survival and reproduction. So when you see these birds zipping in and out of their nests hanging from an outhouse overhang, know that there is a purpose behind their frantic activity.

If you look further out into the sage from the swallows' colony of nests, you will see grazing bison and elk. The large herbivores seem boring at first glance, but if you observe long enough, you may come to appreciate some seemingly odd behaviors.

Chapter 18

Animal Funerals

−.−.−.−.−.−

When animals express their feelings they pour out like water from a
spout. Animals' emotions are raw, unfiltered, and uncontrolled.
Their joy is the purest and most contagious of joys and their grief
the deepest and most devastating. Their passions bring us to our
knees in delight and sorrow.

-Marc Bekoff,
The Emotional Lives of Animals

IT TOOK US SEVERAL MINUTES TO FIGURE OUT WHAT
exactly we were watching. Researchers still do not understand
the underlying evolutionary reasons behind what we observed.
We pulled over to scan the valley floor early one morning. Vet-
eran wildlife watchers use the term "glass" as a verb, meaning
to use binoculars or scopes. We'll stick with "scan." When we
first looked towards the south, we counted five bison that
looked as though they were forming a circle. Occasionally, the
standing bison would take turns dropping their heads into the
interior of the ring. We could see through tiny breaks in the
circle that there was a calf standing next to what looked like a
boulder. We soon learned that boulder was a bison carcass. According to some of the others at the pullout, the cow bison had

fallen over and died during the night. Her calf was still trying to feed. We asked many questions about bison behavior that morning.

Unanswered Questions 18.1
1. Why do adult bison sometimes stand over a bison carcass?
2. At what point do the bison realize that it is too risky to 'guard' the carcass?
3. What happens to a bison calf if its mother dies?

American bison are the most emblematic mammal species in North America. So much so that in 2016 the bison officially became the national mammal. The bison is a member of the bovid family, which split into several species twenty million years ago. Some, like the African cape buffalo and the Asian water buffalo evolved with no hump. Others, like the American bison, gained the large mass of muscle tissue. Their ancestors managed to survive the Pleistocene extinctions that claimed the pronghorn's predators and also the giant mammoths and mastodons. We will discuss the pronghorn and their predators in the next chapter. Eventually, bison became one of the most numerous large mammals that have ever existed. Then, in the 1800s they almost went extinct because of commercial hunting and the introduction of diseases from domestic cattle. In Yellowstone, they fill the valleys. If you take a moment to observe these enormous beauties, they will allow you to peer into their world.

The day they are born, bison calves are on their feet and ready to move. Mothers of some species, like pronghorn, will hide their young and only return to nurse. They do this because their young are not fast enough to outrun predators. Bison mothers don't need to be fast because of their great size. They keep their young with them. Unlike the pronghorn who hide their young, bison use a 'follower strategy.' Cows follow the herd and babies follows their mothers. This herd mentality can easily be seen and experienced while driving through the Lamar Valley. Their strong desire to follow and keep up with the herd has consequences. For you and your vehicle, this may mean that you will have to wait in a bison jam for hours until they all cross the road. For a mother bison, it means deciding whether to stay with the herd or stay with her calf who is struggling behind. Either decision will be costly. This very decision seems to have set the stage for a bizarre event in 2016.

On May 9, 2016, a father and his son pulled into the parking lot at the Lamar Buffalo Ranch demanding to speak with a ranger. The man had picked up a bison calf and put it into the back of his vehicle. According to the man, the calf was alone just off the road and was cold and lost. He felt sorry for it, so he packed it up and drove for help. "We didn't have the heart to, kind of, just leave it there and let it suffer, you know, as the darkness descended," said the man. After unsuccessfully trying to reunite the calf with the herd, park rangers decided to euthanize it. The man received probation.

There are several lessons within this story. The obvious one is that no matter how sad you feel for wild animals you should never attempt to rescue one. Our emotions should never cause us to do something as foolish or dangerous as putting a bison calf in a car. Second, it is possible that this calf was lost or confused or sad (that is if we agree that animals have an emotional state). Finally, the reason the calf was left behind may have been the result of an emotional decision its mother had to make: stay with the herd or remain with the calf. If she decides to move with the herd, she will lose her calf. Staying behind with the calf, though, will cause mother to risk losing the protection that the group provides.

Unanswered Questions 18.2
1. Do animals form friendships?
2. What is the evolutionary basis for this 'mourning' behavior?
3. Are animals aware of the concept of death?
4. Is there an emotional or ritual component to this 'grieving' behavior?
5. Is this strictly a con-specific (within the same species) behavior?

This herd behavior creates strong bonds between adults. Perhaps this is why the adults were standing guard over their fallen friend that morning in the valley. To gain a better understanding, we need to look at examples from various species.

Some birds know when other birds of their same species have died. Western scrub jays have been observed summoning others to screech over the body of a dead jay. One leading researcher in this field of animal emotions states that they simply do not know enough to state that this behavior implies an emotional component, but they cannot rule it out.

In 2010, a mother giraffe was observed standing alongside her dead calf over a span of four days. In 2012, biologists observed a mother giraffe refusing to leave the body of her dead calf. Do giraffes, as well as other animals, have a mental model of death?

Some species of elephants may even recognize the dead and display some form of respectful behavior. African elephants have been shown to exhibit a strong preference for ivory and elephant skulls over other objects. Some even visit the bones of relatives who die within their home range.

Finally, mother chimpanzees have been observed carrying around their dead young for weeks. This unusual behavior may show that chimps understand the concept of death and have ways to cope with it.

Researchers must be careful about not attributing human behaviors to these animals. Still, the animal practices are noteworthy. Comparative research is needed to show whether any other species show similar responses. Also, more research is required to try to figure out if these reactions have any relationships with specific cognitive or social behaviors. There's no doubt that what we observed that morning was a special ceremony.

Peering into the world of bison is one of many things you can do in the Lamar Valley. You can also watch ghosts. These ghosts spend their days napping and stretching, but occasionally you can see them hunt.

Chapter 19

Outrunning Ghosts

— . — . — . — . —

In the hurtling pronghorn, the vanished predators have left behind a heartrending spectacle. Through the smoking displays of wild abandon runs a desperate spirit, resigned to racing pickup trucks in its eternal longing for cheetahs.

-William Stolzenburg,
Where the Wild Things Were

Nebraska Resident Claims He was Stalked by a Cheetah while Riding His Bike

Colorado Family Stay Inside Their House for 4 Days because of a Roaming Elephant

Male Lion Killing Pet Dogs in Missouri Neighborhood

WHAT IF HEADLINES SUCH AS THESE WERE REALITY? Sure, they are a stretch, but the idea of bringing different animals to the central and western sections of the U.S. could be a smart idea. At least, according to some conservation scientists.

It sounds intriguing to bring animals back to the U.S. and, at the same time, help Africa's large mammal population. The idea is to actively promote the restoration of wild vertebrates into North America so that pests and weeds do not eventually dominate. Ecologists refer to this effort as "rewilding," and it would consist of several carefully managed steps.

Phase one would be restoring herbivores such as the Bolson tortoise and using feral horses, Asian asses, and Bactrian camels as proxies for the species that once roamed North America. The second phase would be more controversial as it would introduce African cheetahs, Asian and African elephants, and lions to private properties in the West. Then, phase three would create one or more parks in an area of the Great Plains that is economically depressed. In this park, they would slowly reintroduce these large predators. Riding through Nebraska and seeing lions and cheetahs would be a different experience.

Now, before you write this idea off as crazy, there could be some benefits. Introducing large carnivores could have significicant ecological benefits as the predators would control the herbivores which would increase the growth of vegetation. The introduction of the cheetah would, potentially, impact one animal in Yellowstone in a considerable way.

The North American pronghorn is the only surviving member of its family. The pronghorn family appeared seventeen million years ago with the current species appearing three million years ago. It is often mistakenly referred to as the antelope, probably because of a description of the animal during the Lewis and Clark expedition. The pronghorn is part of a group more closely related to giraffes. Males and females both have horns which are made up of a bony interior covered by a keratin sheath. Unlike antelope, pronghorns shed their horns every year. Along with distinguishable black cheek patches, the bucks have horns with a prong that juts towards the front, thus the name.

Females typically give birth to twins between May and June. They protect their newly born babies by hiding them in vegetation until the young can travel and keep up with the herd. Pronghorns form groups which increases their likelihood to detect predators. When a potential predator is spotted, an individual will flare out its white patch located on its rump. This lets the others know that it is time to flee.

During the 1800s, the pronghorn population numbered thirty-five million in the American West, second only to bison. Unlike bison, pronghorns do not rely on grasses for food. In fact, their most important foods are sagebrush and other shrubs as well as herbaceous plants. They have the unique ability to eat lichens, lupine, and other plants that are toxic to other ungulates. Some researchers think that their large liver removes the plant toxins from their bloodstream. These animals are fascinating to watch as they prance in and around Yellowstone, but it is most exciting to delve into their history.

The pronghorn family flourished in North America as it became highly specialized to live and thrive in the grassland-savanna habitat. For example, members of the family had cheek teeth with high crowns and enamel extending past the gum line, a pattern of dentition called hypsodont. This adaptation kept the teeth from wearing down as they ate, much as it does for cows and horses today. Their eyes are the largest of any North American ungulate in relation to body size. This allows them to detect predators from a great distance. Some research states that they can identify movement four miles away.

Their heart, lungs, and trachea are larger than ungulates of similar body size. Their blood is extremely rich in hemoglobin, the iron-carrying pigment of blood that binds to oxygen. Other adaptations include the reduction of the mass of the distal limbs, the complete loss of the lateral digits, and the reduction of ratios of proximal to distal limb bone sizes. These characteristics groom the pronghorn toward one thing: speed.

The American pronghorn today can reach speeds up to sixty miles per hour but can sustain speeds of forty miles per hour for several miles. In fact, they're so fast that no predator in Yellowstone can come close to catching them. Evolutionary biologists must ask why pronghorns would allocate so much energy in being fast when they do not have to be.

The American West was entirely different 13,000 years ago. Giant ground sloths, which stood over nine feet tall roamed the land. Camels, horses, deer, muskoxen, and several species of bison were plentiful. In addition to these, pronghorns lived alongside some of the most vicious and successful predators North America has ever seen. Short-faced bears, which looked like grizzlies on stilts, were present. Saber-toothed cats, jaguars, lions, and hyenas would have quickly disposed of the pronghorn. Hyenas may have been the most dangerous with their long legs, their ability to shred bone, and their pack behavior. The fauna in North America was more diverse than the modern-day savanna of East Africa. The greatest threat to the pronghorns were the American cheetahs just for the simple fact that they were also sprinters. It's hard to imagine prey animals surviving this period. However, pronghorns stood out. It was their speed that would prove to be vital to their survival. They had to be fast.

Antilocapra, the pronghorn family, experienced four million years of selective pressure to be fast. Biologists call this directional selection. This speed would have been the direct result from an environmental pressure, namely, survival. Pronghorns were selected for traits to avoid the sprinting, stalking, and coursing predators. That selection was relaxed 10,000 years ago when most of its dangerous predators went extinct. In fact, more than sixty North American species weighing over 100 pounds disappeared. Wolves, coyotes, and cougars are the only predators that survive today. The pronghorns in Yellowstone represent a group that has experienced relaxed selection after 5,000 generations. One might think pronghorns should have gotten slower—they would still be able to outrun modern predators. Energy devoted to speed could be used elsewhere. Biologists argue that pronghorns are fast because of their past. One expert argues that we really cannot expect adaptations built by lengthy coevolution to decay so rapidly. They have not had enough time to slow down.

Some ecologists would like to know how pronghorns would be impacted if we bring back a piece of history into their habitat. For example, if we were to bring African cheetahs to the U.S. to pose as the extinct American cheetahs, would they regulate pronghorn populations and thus help stabilize the vegetation? In addition to ecological benefits, the reintroductions may also have socioeconomic benefits.

One prime example of this is Gorongosa National Park in Mozambique. Gorongosa is considered one of the greatest restorations in Africa. Philanthropist Greg Carr invested millions of dollars into the reintroduction and restoration of animals into this refuge that had previously been torn apart by poverty, poaching, and civil war. In 2008, the Carr Foundation formed a twenty-year partnership with the government of Mozambique. Not only did they reintroduce animals to the area, but they educated the residents around the park and helped farmers work through issues, all with the purpose of gaining support. They also created jobs for locals and found ways to generate sustainable revenue for the park. They even gave former poachers jobs as park rangers which took incredible planning and foresight. The research team continues to use science to study the ecosystem so that they can make informed management decisions. Planning the restoration, winning the people, and boosting the economy seem to be the prerequisites to a successful reintroduction.

Although no one has quantified the benefits of Pleistocene rewilding in the U.S., researchers have done this on a regional basis. In 2016, a group of biologists published a paper that attempted to quantify the socioeconomic benefits of cougar reintroduction to the southeastern U.S. Vehicle collisions caused by deer in the U.S. increased 50% from 1990-2004. Deer costs eastern states $3.5 billion annually from damage to crops, nursery plants, and landscaping. Through projections and models, the researchers predicted that cougar recolonization would reduce deer-related accidents by 22% over a thirty-year period. The avoided accidents would result in avoided costs of $50 million annually. The model also predicted that over thirty years, cougars would result in 21,400 fewer injuries and 155 fewer deaths from deer-related accidents. These numbers are based on the prediction that a single cougar would kill 259 deer over an average lifespan of six years.

Rewilding projections and proposals will likely continue to be written and published with an emphasis on conservation. We may eventually see cougars populate the east coast either from intentional recolonization or because of natural migration, but it is unlikely that we will ever see any form of Pleistocene rewilding. As one expert commented, "With sufficient open space, they (pronghorns) will always be there, to remind us of just how fast a North American cheetah could run."

For now, the pronghorns will have to continue sharing space and outrunning their long-time predator, the coyote, who have their own remarkable story to tell.

Chapter 20

Persistence Pays Off

‒ . ‒ . ‒ . ‒ . ‒

The world ain't all sunshine and rainbows. It is a very mean and nasty place and it will beat you to your knees and keep you there permanently if you let it. You, me, or nobody is gonna hit as hard as life. But it ain't how hard you hit; it's about how hard you can get hit, and keep moving forward. How much you can take, and keep moving forward.

-Rocky Balboa

YOU COULD NOT HAVE ASKED FOR A BETTER DAY IN the valley. The air was crisp with a breeze that had a 'bite' to it. No one was complaining because we had plenty of clothes and coffee. However, it did not take us long to realize that all may not be well with the pair of coyotes that we had been observing for the past hour.

The coyotes had suddenly encountered an unwanted visitor in the form of a wolf. This was especially dangerous for a couple of reasons. Gray wolves are much larger and more potent than coyotes, so the pair needed to be cautious. This particular wolf was near the coyotes' den where pups were hiding. As we watched the coyotes attempt to chase and distract the wolf, we wondered aloud about how these two species of canines have interacted, and coevolved, through thousands of years.

Interactions between these carnivores certainly played a role in their evolution. When you have two top predators in an ecosystem, they affect each other. These interactions include both direct and indirect competition. Exploitative competition is an indirect interaction when one species outcompetes another for a shared resource. On the other hand, interference competition is a direct interaction, such as harassment or just outright killing. Both exploitative and interference competition exists between wolves and coyotes, but it is hard to measure how both of these impact the food web dynamics of the two species.

The reason why wolves and coyotes interact is relatively simple; the two have a similar ecological niche. Their diets overlap which creates potential problems for the smaller coyotes. The most intense of these interactions occur around wolf-killed ungulate carcasses in Yellowstone. Coyotes must be careful, but they do have some options. They can avoid wolves by being active at different times, in different areas, or choose to eat different prey.

Yellowstone provided a natural experimental site where researchers could observe, measure, and record aspects of this relationship. Coyotes and wolves had a long history of coexistence until the 1930s when coyotes in Yellowstone found themselves all alone without their larger relative. Federal control programs had exterminated all the wolves. For the next sixty years, coyotes were the top dog. Federal programs successfully got rid of wolves, but scientists were left wondering how coyotes were able to survive and persist. To understand this, we must consider the coyote's past and attempt to understand its behavior.

The coyote of North America, *Canis latrans*, is one of seven (or ten, depending on how you split or lump species) members of the taxonomic genus *Canis* included within the Canidae family. Canidae ancestry can be traced back to a genus of carnivorous mammals named *Miacis*. Species in this genus were about the size of a weasel and appeared during the late Paleocene around fifty-six million years ago. Even though the coyote is actually more primitive than the gray wolf, they both have had a long history of competitive and antagonistic interactions in North America. Therefore, the interaction we witnessed that cold morning in June was nothing new to either of the species.

Wolves hunt in packs and specialize in large prey. They usually rely on tiring out their prey by a long chase. In contrast, coyotes are mainly solitary hunters that kill small mammals by pouncing and shaking them. However, coyotes did not always hunt small mammals. In fact, there is research that shows that during the Pleistocene coyotes hunted and killed larger prey. Pleistocene coyotes were larger than present-day coyotes. It was probably between 11,500 and 10,000 years ago that a decrease in food supply and the megafaunal extinctions led to a shrinkage in coyote size and a niche shift. After animals like sloths, camels, horses, and llamas went extinct, there were fewer prey species for the coyotes to eat. The dire wolf, *Canis dirus*, probably the coyote's most prominent competitor during that time, also became extinct. Being large was not an advantage for coyotes anymore, which is why ecologists observe this shift to smaller coyotes in the fossil record.

Native stories about coyotes tend to focus on their mischievous and cunning behavior as well as their apparent lack of morals. Coyotes have faced intense pressure from hunters, dating back to when Europeans first arrived in North America. Unlike wolves, cougars, and bears, coyotes have adapted and yet thrived in the face of persecution.

During the past several centuries, coyotes have been harassed by and benefited from humans. Coyotes hunted small prey successfully in the western plains of the U.S., but then early settlers pushed west and hunted wolves to extinction and did major damage to other carnivores like mountain lions and bobcats. Coyotes thrived because they reproduced faster than their competitors and were more opportunistic when it came to feeding. The spread of agriculture also played a significant role in coyote expansion. Coyotes had (and still have) no trouble exploiting the environmental changes caused by people.

Coyotes are also considered habitat generalists, meaning they can make their home in woodlands, grasslands, deserts, mountains, agricultural, and urban areas. Territories vary depending on the season, the population in a particular area, as well as pack status. Transient coyotes, or loners, tend to roam more and may establish vast territories. Coyote packs are more likely to form a smaller territory.

Whereas wolves are highly social, coyotes are typically less social. They do exist in packs in some areas. However, they are also found in pairs or as individuals. A "pack" is usually just a mating pair and offspring. Western coyotes tend to be a little smaller and have to avoid top predators like wolves. In places like Yellowstone, wolves have pushed coyotes into areas inhabited by people like campgrounds and roadsides. In the southeast, coyotes compete with gray and red foxes. They are usually dominant over both species, with gray foxes having the advantage over red foxes because they can climb trees. Eastern coyotes, especially, easily adapt to urban areas that are densely populated by humans.

While coyotes have recolonized North America over the last 100 years, there is no doubt that the eastern coyote is a hybrid. What's remarkable is the evolutionary story this creature has to tell. Studies show that the eastern coyote is a mixture of three species: coyote, dog, and wolf. Here's the breakdown by genes of eastern coyotes:

- Genome of coyotes in the Northeast: 60%-84% coyote, 8-25% wolf, and 8%-11% dog

- Genome of coyotes in Virginia: 85% coyote, 2% wolf, and 13% dog

- Genome of coyotes in the deep south: 91% coyote, 4% wolf, and 5% dog

Coyotes now roam throughout most eastern states. For example, they are in every county in North Carolina. They can hunt, eat, sleep, and raise their pups in cities. They are even hunting deer, filling a niche left open by the red wolves (*C.*

lupus rufus) that once roamed the area. A recent study showed that from 2006-2009, coyotes were undoubtedly responsible for 37% of South Carolina's fawn deaths and could have been responsible for as much as 80% of fawn deaths.

Typically, they are most active during the early morning and late evening hours, making them crepuscular. Because of their opportunistic attitude, coyotes may roam throughout the day. In areas of high human activity, like urban environments, coyotes become more nocturnal to avoid conflict. They have the amazing ability to remain unseen by moving where terrain provides them the most cover. They have excelled at surviving.

When it comes to feeding, coyotes are known as ecological generalists. As their range expanded, so did their diet. Coyotes eat all sorts of food, including meat, fruits and vegetables, nuts, carrion, and even trash. They have been known to eat pet food off of porches. A significant portion of eastern coyotes' diet consists of small mammals, like rodents and rabbits, insects, fruits, and nut crops.

To show the impact of urban coyotes, the Urban Coyote Program is a long-term research project that began in the Chicago metropolitan areas in 2000 "as a non-biased attempt to address shortcomings in urban coyote ecology information and management." The following are some major implications that this program lists from its research:

> As a top predator, coyotes are performing an essential role in the Chicago region., such as controlling rodent, deer, and Canada goose populations.

Coyotes in urban environments switch their activity patterns to be more active at night when human activity is minimal.
Most coyotes are feeding on typical prey items, such as rodents and rabbits, and avoiding trash.
Wildlife feeding will eventually habituate some coyotes, leading to conflicts.
Coyotes appear to be monogamous.
Coyotes are exposed to a wide range of diseases; however, to date, none of them pose a serious human health risk.
Effective control programs target nuisance coyotes, rather than targeting the general coyote population. Coyotes removed through lethal control efforts or other causes are quickly replaced.
Some individuals exhibit dangerous behavior and should be removed from the population.

Eastern coyotes, especially those that live and persist in urban habitats, tend to frighten people. Learning about these predators and understanding the research may help people as they live with them. Below are some common questions that many people have about this animal. Some of these issues are specific to the eastern coyotes. These answers are not only supported by journal articles, but also by an undergraduate research project at Mitchell Community College (NC). Student researchers used trail cameras from 2012-2017 to learn about coyote behaviors and movement patterns throughout an urban area. Hopefully, some of the answers will help clear up misconceptions.

1) Have coyotes just recently learned to live with people? Nope.

In a recent news article, a North Carolina Wildlife Resources Commission biologist stated that coyotes are "getting used to people." This quote makes it sound like the co-existence between coyotes and humans is relatively recent. It's not. Coyotes have never been solely wilderness creatures. For the 15,000 years since humans have inhabited North America, coyotes have been living alongside us. Besides, we do not ever want coyotes to get used to us to the point where they feel comfortable.

2) Are coyotes "non-native" and "invasive"? If you remember our discussion from chapter fifteen, it depends on how you define "non-native." As far as invasive goes, not by a long shot.

It is probably accurate to say that coyotes are the most persecuted animal in North America, with 500,000 of them killed every year. What makes them different than any other urban animal is that they are deemed a "problem" just because of their presence. Most accounts describe coyotes as "non-native" and "invasive." Those are two words that may not be suitable in this case. In 2008, an Iredell County (NC) Animal Services and Control publication stated that at one point in the past, foxes were in so much demand for hunting that someone transported coyotes from Virginia into Iredell County to replace them. Hurricane Hugo, which came through the county in 1989, supposedly demolished the coyote pens, and they all escaped into the wild. Judging by how fast coyotes have spread into other counties throughout North Carolina, it is unclear whether this single event helped coyotes move into the area faster than they normally would have. Even though coyotes may not have always inhabited North Carolina, red wolves once did. Since recent genetic research has shown that 80% of the red wolf genome is similar to coyotes, you could make an argument that coyotes (their genes, anyway) are native.

3) **Do coyotes pose a danger to pets?** Apparently, yes, but conflicts are rare.

Occasionally, coyotes do kill pets, but it is hardly a common occurrence. Contrary to popular belief, coyotes do not merely eat garbage and harass pets. It's not the dumpsters or the small cats that attract coyotes to urban areas. Coyotes are top-level carnivores and actively engaged as predators. Most conflicts with pets are because coyotes view small dogs and cats as competitors, not as food. In fact, this aggressive response is similar to the reaction that coyotes show towards smaller foxes. Coyotes in urban ecosystems do not depend on pets as food. If they did, we would not have any pets left. In most studies, cats only make up 1-2% or less of the diet of urban coyotes. Our studies have shown that coyotes prefer cottontails in Iredell County.

4) Are coyotes dangerous to humans in urban environments? Typically, not at all.

Coyotes have been documented attacking people. In 1981, a small child died from a coyote attack. One 2009 study classified 142 U.S. and Canadian coyote attack reports. They categorized the attacks as follows:

- Predatory- 37%
- Investigative- 22%
- Pet-related- 6%
- Defensive- 4%
- Rabid- 7%

Most of the attacks occurred during the pup-rearing season (May-July). Problem coyotes seem to be those that have become habituated to humans. We have mentioned that urban coyotes avoid humans by shifting to more nocturnal activities. Our data indicate this. Over 126 days, we collected fifty-six independent coyote captures on our cameras within city limits. Our data show that coyotes within city limits are, on average, 68% nocturnal. Four capture sites in one particular area showed that coyotes were 89% nocturnal.

Habituation could be the result of intentional or unintentional feeding of wildlife. To successfully live with these predators, it is always best to yell and scream at them if you see them in your neighborhood. Make sure they stay wild, but also make sure they stay nervous.

5) Are coyotes frequently reported as rabid wildlife species? Nope.

Rabies is a common fear among those of us that live in the city. The Center for Disease Control reports that raccoons account for most of the rabies outbreaks in the U.S., followed by bats, skunks, and foxes. Unlike raccoons, coyote-strain rabies (except for a tiny population in South Texas) has not been an issue in the U.S. However, raccoon-strain rabies or raccoon rabies virus can spillover into coyote populations. This has happened only occasionally.

6) Can you ever get rid of all the coyotes? It doesn't look like it.

If a pest-control company tells you they can eliminate coyotes, they can't (at least not permanently). Most predators are either solitary (mountain lions) or social (gray wolves), but not both— except coyotes. Coyotes can also catch a variety of prey, from small mice to deer. These are just some of the characteristics that allow them to live just about anywhere. Also, coyotes seem to be somewhat immune to exploitation. One study from 1999 showed that unexploited coyote populations tend to have

older age structure, high adult survival rates, and low reproductive rates. However, in highly exploited populations,
coyotes are characterized by younger age structures, lower
adult survival rates, and increased percentages of yearlings reproducing and increased liter sizes. What can you do?
Removal programs that target problem coyotes on an individual basis may be more cost-effective. It is important to
remember how you define 'problem.' Not all individual coyotes
are problems just because of their presence.

7) Are coyotes beneficial to urban ecosystems? Yes.

Coyotes may be the top predator in some urban ecosystems.
In some areas, coyotes may act as keystone species and help
regulate populations of other animals. In the absence of coyotes in fragmented landscapes, mesopredator (like raccoons or
cats) populations increase. When mesopredators increase,
songbirds tend to decrease, so you could make the argument
that coyotes benefit native songbirds. Coyotes can also influence foxes, cats, raccoons, and skunks through direct
competition. They may even affect behavior in domestic cats
in urban environments. Domestic cats may kill as many as four
billion native birds per year in the U.S. One recent study shows
that coyotes may help native bird populations by eliminating
cats from specific areas, or at least causing cats to avoid certain
areas.

Coyotes, when they are living without any pressure from
wolves, tend to show that they are capable of being a top predator. They benefit ecosystems, they reproduce and adapt to

their surroundings, and they persist. Coyotes that live with wolves also seem to change and endure. Following wolf reintroduction, coyote densities in northeastern Yellowstone declined 39%. This decline reached 50% within the first three years of the wolf reintroduction. Presumably, this decrease was a result of pressure from the new predator and competitor. The wolf population has since stabilized, but coyotes remain the most abundant carnivore.

Chapter 21

Reintroduction Interactions

−.−.−.−.−.−

These individual populations [of starfish] are the keystone of the community's structure, and the integrity of the community and its unaltered persistence through time, that is, stability, are determined by their activities and abundances.

- Robert Paine

EVEN THOUGH IT WAS JUNE, THE COMBINATION OF the wind and the setting sun kept the temperature hanging steadily at 40° F. We were standing up on a hill looking over a broad swath of sage. I'll never forget when it happened. Every animal we had observed that evening had been magnificent, but they would not compare to the drama that was about to unfold. Sandhill cranes were standing along the river to the south, pronghorn and bison scattered throughout, and a pair of bald eagles were perched high in a nearby cottonwood. Suddenly, we heard a lone wolf howl from the north. Multiple howls from the south soon followed this single howl. We were listening to members of the Druid wolf pack which, at that time, controlled most of the northern range of Yellowstone.

They soon came into view and continued howling. I saw the students' eyes light up with excitement. One student said softly, "This is what I've been waiting for my whole life!"

Fourteen wolves first came to Yellowstone in 1995, and seventeen more in 1996. Wolf reintroduction started long before that, however. On December 28, 1973, the Endangered Species Act was signed to protect species that were endangered or threatened. Since the gray wolf fit this description, wildlife officials listed it as endangered the following year, and wolf recovery was mandated. Congress, though, did not appropriate money for a wolf recovery environmental impact statement (EIS) until 1991. An EIS is a required federal document that describes the pros and cons of the proposed environmental action, in this case bringing wolves into the U.S. from Canada. The EIS was completed in 1994, and then a period of public feedback began. Finally, the wolves arrived. It is easy to overlook how many battles had to be fought for wolves to get here, conflicts that are still on-going today. When we recognize these struggles, we can appreciate the people involved even more.

On the morning of April 24, 1995, Chad McKittrick ran to his truck, grabbed his *Ruger 7 millimeter*, settled the rifle butt against his shoulder, took aim at an animal, and fired a shot. This was a shot that would officially start years of controversy that remain unresolved. The animal at the other end of the bullet was not just any animal.

Chad and his friend, Dusty, had traveled down a dirt road right off of Bear Creek Highway to pull a truck out of the mud that had gotten stuck the day before. They packed lumber, chains, shovels, axes, pry bars, a jack, and as Chad put it, his "just-in-case firepower," a *.44 caliber magnum revolver*, a *.22 rifle*, and the *Ruger 7mm*. You never know when you may need protection, especially in the forests of southern Montana in April. As the two men worked to get the truck free, Dusty whispered, "Chad, look," as he pointed up the hill at something moving. Chad responded, "That's a wolf, Dusty. I'm going to shoot it."

About 450 feet away, a big, dark gray wolf was strolling along a ridgeline, silhouetted clearly against the sky. This wolf, which researchers had collared and named #10, was one of the fourteen Canadian wolves brought to Yellowstone in 1995. Wolves are assigned numbers based on their radio collar. He had been released into the wild a month before this encounter with Chad. He was the largest and boldest of the bunch. If a wolf ever did look like an alpha, it was #10. In fact, before being released, he was introduced to female wolf #9 in an acclimation pen in the park. At the point he met his end by the bullet, she was ready to den and have pups.

One would think that, because wolves are highly social animals, this illegal shooting of wolf #10 would result in the loss of his entire family. However, park officials recaptured the family and held them in an enclosure throughout the summer. During the fall, they were all released, with a bonus. Male wolf #8, who had been a wild wolf on his own, was waiting outside the pen with hopes of becoming wolf #9's new mate and the pups newly adopted father. In fact, the pups wasting no time accepting wolf #8, as they were seen nipping, barking, and pulling on his tail. The willingness to adopt offspring that have been sired by another male is rare in the mammal world. One of those male pups, wolf #21, actually took five pups that were not his and became an alpha male himself. Thus, wolf #9 put the Yellowstone wolf population back on the map.

Wolf #21 spent a little over two years with his mother, #9, before venturing out to become the alpha male of another pack. We were watching and listening to several descendants of #21 that evening in the valley. He fathered pups every year from 1998–2004, including twenty pups in 2000. Wolf #21 became a legend to wolf-watchers, not only because of his size but also because of his calm and gentle spirit. Alphas typically eat first and will defend their right against others. He was often seen walking away from a kill he had just made so that he could urinate or take a nap. This would allow the younger wolves to take their fill. Wolf #21 also was seen playing with the young wolves and letting them climb on top of him, much like a human father might do when wrestling with his young sons. Rick McIntyre, a biological technician for the Yellowstone Wolf Project, describes #21 the following way:

"When pups harassed him by biting his tail or ears, #21 would often just walk away; I once saw him cross the road and hide in some bushes to get away from pups that were bothering him. Of course, he also used his great size and strength to benefit his pack. If the younger wolves were attacking an elk, but could not pull it down, #21 would run in and help bring it down."

Wolf #21 died in 2004, which made him an exceptionally long-lived wild wolf. He left quite a legacy. In 2001, his pack numbered thirty-seven, the largest known wolf pack in history. Many of his pups went on to either join or start other packs.

Since wolves like #10 and #9 arrived, they have been the focus of intense ecology-based research. Wolves are referred to as keystone species, just like the cutthroat trout. They help regulate ecosystems from the top as apex predators. In theory, more wolves mean less elk, which means more trees for many other species. This argument is not new to science.

In the 1960s, Robert Paine began prying starfish off of rocks and tossing them into the ocean as far as he could. In doing so, he was testing the importance of predators in ecosystems. Paine's research helped support an idea that his former instructor (and colleagues) had developed. It is called the green world hypothesis and is still applicable to ecology today. This theory states that ecosystems are regulated from the top-down. Predators control herbivores, which leads to vegetation growth. It's a different approach to the standard bottom-up food chains that show that plants get energy from the sun, and then feed the herbivores, which, in turn, feed the carnivores. Paine's conclusions did not disprove bottom-up regulation. They just added another dimension, that of predator regulation. Two new terms came from these early experiments: trophic cascades and keystone species. So, Paine's theory predicted that having wolves in the area would limit elk growth, and therefore, increase aspen/cottonwood stands and eventually help songbird/insect/beaver populations.

Many conservationists and biologists thought wolves were going to solve multiple problems. The hope was that wolves would regulate the elk populations. The elk had increased in number because, without wolves, they had no natural predators. This increase was a problem because the elk were not allowing cottonwood and aspen trees to mature. Since 1995, elk numbers have gone down, but not as much as researchers had hoped. However, in some areas, aspen trees seem to be doing better. Since elk numbers are still high in the park, some ecologists have come up with a new theory called "fear ecology." This means that elk will not graze for long periods of time in areas that are occupied by wolves. The elk just become more vigilant. There have been decreases in elk density in certain areas. Since wolves came back, beaver colonies have increased because of the availability of aspen and cottonwood trees. One recent paper even shows that having more wolves in the area cause grizzly bears to browse more serviceberries, thus causing direct competition with elk, since they also browse on this vegetation. These two types of deciduous trees are essential to many species including songbirds, insects, and beavers.

Another explanation why elk populations are not decreasing as much as researchers predicted could be that there has not been an adequate amount of time. We typically want quick results, and in this case, it just may not be possible. What if, instead of using the elk overpopulation problem to justify having wolves in an ecosystem, we focused on more immediate benefits? For example, more wolves mean more carcasses, and more carcasses benefit everyone.

Before the wolf reintroduction, the majority of carrion/carcass buildup would be at the end of winter. Elk, deer, and bison struggle during the harsh winter months and some die from starvation. As we stated in chapter twelve, this concentration of carrion is not suitable for maintaining a healthy scavenger population because most of the meat ends up rotting. The scavengers cannot eat fast enough. It is much more advantageous if the carcasses are spread out throughout the year. That's what having efficient predators, like wolves, do for an ecosystem. Elk carcasses can be found in all seasons now that wolves are back. This helps both large and small predators.

Human hunting also leaves too much accumulation of meat. For comparison, from November to May, wolves provide an average of 29,000 pounds of meat for scavengers scattered throughout. From January to mid-February, hunters provide about 73,000 pounds of meat. That's too concentrated to help the scavengers in any way. There are also conservation implications here. Ravens, eagles, and other birds of prey usually eat the excess accumulation of meat. When birds of prey are attracted to an area where they normally would not hunt (spillover), there could be problems. For example, ravens tend to feed on the eggs of the endangered sage grouse. If ravens are attracted to areas where the grouse have eggs, this could significantly impact the grouse population. So, wolves directly help scavengers of all sizes by killing prey all year long and thus scattering the carcasses.

These wolf-kill carcasses also benefit many overlooked species, the invertebrates. We cannot exclude the invertebrate carrion ecosystem if we want to completely understand how predator-prey interactions (like wolves and elk) affect ecosystem functioning. One fascinating study done in Yellowstone specifically looked at how elk and bison carcasses impacted beetle communities. Data sets from both 1978 and 1993 showed that 445 different species of beetle took advantage of kill sites. This included 23,365 individuals. Beetles showed up in higher numbers at the carcass sites when compared to control sites without carcasses. The most common carcass-associated beetle was a silphid species, *Thanatophilus lapponicus*. At elk carcasses, 2730 individual silphids were collected, with none being collected from control plots. As far as bison carcass plots, 4958 individuals were found. Four were found at control plots. The beetles were congregating near the food.

This study was just dealing with beetle diversity. Think about all the other insects, bacteria, and fungi present at carcass sites. To my knowledge, there has not been a study to document all the species that benefit from a large vertebrate carcass in Yellowstone. This type of study is probably not practical. Yes, wolves are impacting the ecosystem and helping out species, but we may never know their actual impact. Maybe we should turn from looking at elk and narrow our focus to the invertebrates or even the microbes.

Predators are important. Regulation of ecosystems is essential. Yellowstone has unlimited value.

Part Five: Unsolicited Advice

The Roosevelt Arch sits at the north entrance of Yellowstone.

Chapter 22

Arrival

–.–.–.–.–

Paradise Valley

LOW VISIBILITY AND HIGH WINDS MAKE LANDING IN Bozeman, MT interesting. When the plane drops below the clouds, and the snow-covered mountains appear out of nowhere, you get the feeling an adventure is about to begin. Once the rental cars are acquired, and baggage claimed, we aim south toward the oldest and most majestic of all the national parks, Yellowstone.

You'll need supplies. Our first stop out of the airport is Walmart in Bozeman, which is a mix of college students, tourists, and folks that are making their monthly trip from the vast wilderness to get their supplies. Three or four meals and several snacks that will comfortably fit in a day pack are all you need at this point. Trail mix, peanut butter and jelly, a loaf of bread, fruit, and tuna are popular choices. Most participants carry a reusable water bottle along with them in their pack. After thirty minutes of shopping, we are on our way, via I-90 towards Livingston, MT where we will access U.S. 89.

Once we exit I-90, or as we like to call it "The Autobahn" with a speed limit of eighty miles per hour, Paradise Valley awaits. Farms and ranches line the road on the way to the north entrance of the park. We'll make our first educational stop in the heart of this valley at the most beautiful rest area in the world. This just happens to be a great place to discuss the issues concerning the river brought on by development, farming, ranching, and tourism. Fortunately, this valley is still here, as there were several attempts to dam the river and flood the valley. As recent as the 1970s, some activists wanted to dam the river to provide electric power and irrigation to the surrounding areas.

Mammoth

Gardiner, MT is a welcome sight because it sits at the north entrance of our destination. By the time we reach it, most of us are exhausted from a long travel day. If there's time, we will make our way to Mammoth through the Roosevelt Arch, a huge stone structure, which had its cornerstone laid in 1903 by President Theodore Roosevelt.

Approximately five miles south of the arch lies Mammoth Hot Springs. The hot springs are located on a hill of travertine located adjacent to Fort Yellowstone and the Mammoth Hot Springs Historic District. Wooden walkways mark the way around and through the cliffs of travertine, with the smell of sulfur in the air. It is critical to stay on the sidewalks because the ground beneath is unstable. It is not uncommon to see bears, elk, bison, deer, and even the occasional bull snake.

Several years ago, we were exploring the springs when a black bear decided to pass behind us at forty yards. Two tourists started chasing after the bear on foot yelling something we believed to be in French. They looked as if they were attempting to get a picture and they wanted the bear to stop and pose. We had a guide that day, a female park ranger, who turned around and said in a loud voice, "Do not chase the bear, it will eat you." I guess some people need to hear that bears could eat them. The park requires that visitors maintain a 100-yard distance from all predatory animals, and a twenty-five-yard distance from grazing animals. It may look like you are entering a petting zoo with the elk laying around resting after gorging on the beautifully manicured grass, but these animals are wild and, therefore, potentially dangerous.

While in Mammoth be sure and check out the visitor center, enjoy an ice cream cone, and shop for souvenirs.

Roosevelt

Roosevelt Lodge sits an hour east of Mammoth. It was built in 1920 and is located near a former campsite of President Roosevelt. Rustic cabins are available to rent with amenities such as beds, electricity, and wood burning stoves for heat. The property includes heated bathhouses with toilets and showers. The walls of the cabins are thin, making it easy to hear animals during the night. A headlamp or flashlight is a good idea to help you make your way to the bath house in the dark and cold early morning hours.

Temperatures in Yellowstone commonly get down to 30° F at night in June, so pot belly stoves come in handy, as long as you (or better yet, your cabinmate) get up several times a night to stoke the fire. We get up early and stay out late in our Yellowstone classroom. One morning, our alarm went off at 5:00 a.m., but I had been awake for an hour already. I was afraid to move, because I thought it was possible that the sheets surrounding my body had frozen, and I was lying on the only warm section of the bed. Neither of us had stoked the fire during the night.

Fortunately, Roosevelt Lodge is warm with a great restaurant that serves breakfast, lunch, and dinner. We were having breakfast one particular morning when a mother black bear with two cubs strolled between the parking lot and main road close to the huge rustic glass windows in front of our table. We had a front row seat to one of nature's beautiful creatures. Seconds later, the bear made a sound which sent the cubs up a tree. The sow proceeded to walk to a meadow just beside the parking lot. Then she pounced right and disappeared into the tall grass. We heard a yell as she popped back into view with a mule deer fawn in her powerful jaws. The bear carried the carcass toward the tree where her cubs were hiding. They immediately descended and joined her for breakfast. Everyone needs a good meal to start a long day in Yellowstone.

Chapter 23

Northern Range

−.−.−.−.−

Yellowstone Picnic Area

WORKING OUR WAY FROM ROOSEVELT LODGE ON U.S. 212 westbound, there's a popular hiking trail known as the Specimen Ridge Trail, a trail that spans the length of the ridge and ends in the Lamar Valley. We like to hike a short section of this trail because it gives us the opportunity to enjoy wildlife and beautiful panoramic views. The trail also connects to the Yellowstone Picnic Area Trail, a favorite of past participants. Pack a lunch for this hike and be sure to bring your binoculars. It's a four-mile loop with breath-taking views of the Yellowstone River. There will be plenty of opportunities to see pronghorn, bighorn sheep, and bison. Towards the end of the hike, we will walk through a wooded area which makes excellent habitat for the Western Tanager, one of the prettiest birds in North America. There is cell service at the overlook to make calls. Finally, be sure to dress in layers as the wind can be brutal.

Slough Creek

Roughly seven and a half miles from Roosevelt Lodge is an inconspicuous gravel road that leads to Slough Creek Campground. In the early years of the trip, this campground quickly rose to fame with our groups because it is one of the few places with cell phone service and toilets. It is also a great place to view wildlife. We've spotted many wolves and grizzly bears while taking a 'pit' stop.

Lamar Valley

A few miles further east, the rugged terrain opens up into one of the best valleys in the world. The Lamar Valley is approximately eight miles long and three to four miles wide. This valley is believed to be second to only the Serengeti Plain as one of the best places to view wildlife. It's possible to see all of the park's abundant wildlife in this one location, and our group spends a lot of time in this area just watching.

A few years ago, wolves killed a bison during the night, and that kill signaled dinner for many of the different animals in the park. The next morning, we viewed a grizzly lying on the carcass eating his fill while wolves, coyotes, bald eagles, and ravens waited their turn. Getting through the valley can be a challenge at times as bison herds meander slowly along without consideration for cars. Bison jams are a common occurrence along this stretch of road, and if a 2000-pound bison decides to stop and rest on the double yellow lines, there is nothing you can do but wait.

On the eastern edge of the valley is a pull-out with bathrooms called "Hitching Post." Short sagebrush surrounds this area and makes good hunting for local badgers. In fact, we witnessed a badger on the hunt one year. This badger's concentration would not be broken, not even by cars full of tourists taking pictures and stopping in the middle of the road. The badger crossed the road, jumped in the air, and landed on something. Judging by the high pitched squeal heard throughout the car, we could only assume it was a ground squirrel.

Trout Lake

Closer to the northeast entrance of the park, we will stop at Trout Lake, a small twelve-acre lake. This beautiful body of water is home to spawning cutthroat trout, which could easily be caught by just reaching in and grabbing one if park rules allowed. It is a short but steep hike up (and then down) to the lake, but is worth every step.

There's also a strong possibility to get a close view of river otters. We watched as one dove down for what seemed like an eternity only to return to the surface with a huge trout. The otter then rolled over on its back to float while it feasted on the delicacy. Trout Lake is a great location for expert topics and group photos, so bring your cameras.

Thunderer trailhead

One of our favorite stops along this northern road is a short quarter-mile hike down to the banks of Soda Butte Creek. The bravest of trip goers plunge their tired feet into the frigid 38° F water for relief. Often, a fun competition unfolds, and the participants compete to see who can keep their feet in the longest. The winner receives a coveted prize from our leader (a firm pat on the back).

Years ago after drying our numb feet, we gathered at the bank of the creek for one of our expert topic presentations. Out of nowhere a cow moose and her calf wandered out behind us to partake in the wet vegetation. The scream of "Moose!" sent the pair sprinting away. It's important to always keep a soft tone of voice throughout the entire park because you never know when wildlife may be lurking around the corner.

The banks of Soda Butte Creek are also a great location to set up a spotting scope and gaze up high to the elevation of

10,495 feet. We often spot mountain goats nonchalantly navigating the cliffs, unaware that one wrong step means certain death. Bring your binoculars on this short hike for you are sure to see something special.

Cooke City

Approximately five miles outside the northeast entrance to the park lies the not so sleepy town of Cooke City, MT which doubles as our home base. Cooke City has a variety of restaurants, including a gourmet breakfast served out of a snowmobile repair shop, pizza in a saloon, and the famous "Cheddar Bomb" burger served with a huckleberry milkshake. The town also has stores where you can quickly stock up on essentials and find souvenirs for the family. Cooke City also serves as our gateway to the Beartooth Mountains.

Hiking in the Beartooths

We've built significant relationships with several folks in and out of Yellowstone National Park. Fortunately, Dan is one of those people. A wildlife photographer and seasoned naturalist, Dan has a vast knowledge of the Yellowstone ecosystem and the surrounding Beartooth Mountains. He is always gracious enough to let our group tag along as he checks various locations. We never know what we will run into while hiking with Dan. We have seen bears, wolves, mountain goats, foxes, and even the rarely seen Great Gray owls and cute but fierce pine martin.

Once while following Dan up the side of a mountain in the Beartooths (off the trail, of course), we arrived at a large empty nest. Everyone quietly wondered why we needed to stop for that. Dan pointed at a perfectly camouflaged great grey owl perched on an adjacent tree. Then we glanced at another tree opposite the nest, and three chicks were staring at us. I can only imagine what the chicks were thinking as they stared at us: *What are these two-legged creatures that just hiked a mile through the wet grass and mosquito infested bog to stop right at the base of our home?* Dan knew they would be there because he had been following their progress since the mother and father owls made this nest their home the previous March. He camped at the base of this tree with a film crew getting footage for a documentary that he showed us when we returned to his gallery/home.

Kind is an understatement when you describe Dan and his wife, Cindy. Sometimes cookies and coffee await us back at his gallery. He often tells stories of his adventures in photography and film. Fantastic photos of wildlife fill his gallery, but when Dan is there, stories also fill his house. They offer free shipping back to your home if you decide to purchase one.

Oh, and some fierce pine martins live around his house so beware. They frequently wonder up to check out the commotion when we arrive and stampede into Dan's sanctuary. Here are a few tips for hiking with Dan:

1) Keep up. Dan is a walking Google search engine, and you never know what he is going to notice or say. If you are too far behind him, you might miss something interesting

2) Stay quiet. If the group sounds like a herd of bison walking through the wood, the chances of seeing wildlife decrease.

3) Bring your binoculars, camera, and water. Chances are we are going to be off the trail which means that we will probably come upon a bull bison right in our path, so we will have to walk out of our way to get to our destination. That is a true story.

4) Ask questions. Remember the Google reference above.

Wildlife Watching

We spend one of our earliest mornings with Nathan Varley, owner of a wildlife touring company called The Wild Side, LLC. He also serves as the editor of Yellowstone Reports (www.yellowstonereports.com), which is a great site to keep up with all things in Yellowstone. Nathan grew up in Yellowstone in the tiny community of Mammoth Hot Springs. His parents have been biologists and park rangers, living and working in the park for three decades. The park was his backyard and trips with Nathan have proved to be some of the best for wildlife viewings. We have watched female grizzlies with cubs of the year, a wolf den filled with pups, the nests of bald eagles, osprey, great horned owls, and red-tailed hawks. Nathan always seems to know where to go.

Wolf Behavior

When it comes to wolves, Rick is the expert. Rick has been watching wolves with the Wolf Project in Yellowstone since the wolves first arrived. While driving through the Lamar Valley if you see a large group of people with spotting scopes set up, there is a good chance Rick is in the middle. Rick does not just receive information from his team throughout the park via radio, but he also freely shares his knowledge with the crowd by telling interesting stories about the ups and downs of wolf life, who has taken over as various pack leaders, which wolves have had pups, and which ones have died. Rick knows the wolves. When Rick is talking, you will have to listen carefully. He does not speak loudly, but his calm and pleasant demeanor convey his heartfelt love for every wolf. They are his family.

Chapter 24

Grand Loop

-.-.-.-.-.-

Mount Washburn

YOU WILL SOON ENTER A DIFFERENT WORLD AS YOU drive south from Roosevelt. This winding road takes you past Tower Junction and Tower Falls, and then up close to the high peak of Mt. Washburn. This trail is the most strenuous and most rewarding hike of the trip if scenic views are your idea of a reward. There are two routes to the fire tower at the peak of Mt. Washburn. One starts from the parking lot at Dunraven Pass. This way is a little over six miles, round-trip, with a 1400 ft. gain in elevation. This trail will often stay snow-covered until mid to late June. The other route is on the back side of the mountain along a gravel park service road. This trail is six miles round-trip. Both hikes are strenuous, but both have scenic views and are worth tackling for the payoff.

You should dress in layers because temperatures can vary greatly. You could go from sweating to freezing in minutes, and the wind can be rough, so wear a windproof outer shell. Bring plenty of water because there is no water at the top. The low humidity and high winds can suck the water out of your body and cause dehydration. You will want to pack a lunch to eat in the viewing area of the fire tower, which sits at the top. On a clear day, you can see the Grand Canyon of the Yellowstone, Hayden Valley, and the Grand Tetons. Our group usually gets spread out during this hike because of different fitness levels and hiking paces. Don't worry about it, though. If you're in the back of the pack, our motto of 'no one left behind' holds true. There will be plenty of time to take in the scenery no matter what time you make it to the top. Bighorn sheep, yellow-bellied marmots, and golden-mantled ground squirrels call this area home, so bring your binoculars and camera.

Canyon

Canyon Village and the Grand Canyon of the Yellowstone are located just south of Mt. Washburn. The canyon is 800-1400 ft. deep and up to 4000 ft. wide in some places. The Yellowstone River carved this canyon. The Lower Falls is 308 ft. tall, which is more than twice the height of Niagara Falls. Along with the beautiful canyon and falls comes Canyon Village. This tourist development has restaurants, a visitor's center, and a souvenir store. This is an excellent place to buy gifts for your family and friends at home and grab a good meal.

Hayden Valley

The landscape changes further south and the mountains seem to transform and disappear into a thick forest of lodge-pole pines. The winding road straightens and opens up into the Hayden Valley, named for Ferdinand Hayden who led a geological survey of Yellowstone in 1871. Hayden Valley was a natural route to Yellowstone Lake as trappers, explorers, and natives made their way up the Yellowstone River.

An arm of Yellowstone Lake once filled this valley which is why it contains fine-grained lake sediments made of clay, silt, and sand covered with glacial till. The till contains clay which plugs the soil and prevents water from soaking into the ground. This is why the Hayden Valley is swampy and looks different from the Lamar Valley.

If you are into birds, this is the place for you. The valley is also suitable for finding bears, wolves, coyotes, eagles, elk, and of course bison.

There is a mud volcano on the other side of the Hayden Valley. Clever but literal members of the 1870 Washburn expedition named it "Mud Volcano" because of the cone-shaped mud that covered the feature. At some point between 1870-1872, an explosion blew the mud away to reveal it exactly as you will see it today. Acidity is the driving factor here. Hydrosulfide gas is converted to sulfuric acid by microbes. The sulfuric acid breaks down the rock. The release of gasses produces the bubbling that you see here. We recommend holding your breath.

Dragon's Mouth Spring is just a short walk up the board-walk from Mud Volcano. Mostly, it is a sulfur cauldron with a pH between one and two, making it one of the most acidic and fascinating features in the park.

Once through the Hayden Valley we enter the Yellowstone Lake area. Yellowstone Lake is the largest high-altitude lake in North America, and the views of the snowcapped mountains cradling this vast body of water are unforgettable.

Old Faithful and Grand Prismatic

Besides the two thermal features just discussed, Grand Prismatic and Old Faithful stand out. Grand Prismatic is a hot spring located off U.S. Highway 191 on the grand loop and is a sight to behold. This hot spring is colorful, but you wouldn't know it from the boardwalk. A short drive past the Grand Prismatic parking lot you can find the Grand Prismatic Over-look Trail. This trail is less than a mile and gradually climbs 105 ft. to an overlook point so that visitors can take in the majesty of hot spring without many risks. In the past, steep, natural paths weaving through fallen lodgepole pines were used to get to a viewing area.

When you think of Yellowstone National Park, more than likely the first thing that comes to mind is Old Faithful. This geyser draws millions of visitors every year, and the development around Old Faithful is proof. Souvenir shops, restaurants, a visitor center, and the historic inn are some of the spots to visit while in the Old Faithful area. We will spend enough time here for you to explore, shop and watch the geyser erupt.

Chapter 25

Playing in Wild Places

– . – . – . – . –

WE HOPE THAT THESE STORIES WILL SHED LIGHT on the amazing things Yellowstone has to offer. There is a much larger and more important story that Yellowstone, and all other wild places, have to tell. In fact, these wild areas are not just telling the story. They are shouting the story. It is a story about the interconnectedness of play and nature.

The Roosevelt Arch at the north entrance of the park says, "For the Benefit and Enjoyment of the People." The "people" means you and me. This park is for everyone. Wild ecosystems are for everyone. We encourage you to enjoy this park in two main ways: 1) By recreating in the park and 2) By experiencing the closeness of nature. These two are not unrelated. Yellowstone offers these opportunities, but so do backyards, urban streets, and city parks.

We recreate by hiking, jogging, meandering, and snowmobiling. Sometimes we stay on trails. Sometimes we go off-trail. Really what we are doing is playing. Playing in nature is an essential part of our daily lives. For American pronghorn, play begins early in life. A young pronghorn will reach its peak play at about four weeks of age. Playtime includes a heavy dose of running (sprinting). Running and playing as a fawn, however, come with risks. For fawns, play represents around 20% of total energy expenditure. This type of energy expenditure can leave them vulnerable to predation. If there is so much risk involved, why do they continue to sprint, leap, and twist during playtime? Why do they risk so much and leave themselves exposed? Fawns sprint because play is practice for their adult lives. Playful pronghorn fawns will one day grow into the fastest land mammals in North America. They can easily outrun their predators. Pronghorns are made to run. They cannot afford to stand still. Moving is not only a good thing; it's a matter of life and death.

Humans do not have to worry about being chased by giant predators, but some biologists have made the case that we, too, are made to run and play in nature. Bernd Heinrich, who we met earlier, argues this very point in his book, *Why We Run*. Heinrich takes a natural history approach by comparing running and moving in multiple species across the biological spectrum. His central point is that we were once forced to be continually active to find food and survive, and because of this, humans never had the chance to be idle. Unfortunately, we are now often idle for long periods of time. We don't explore the wilderness. We don't go for walks. We don't run. We are content just to sit inside and watch the television or play video games or stare at a social media feed.

We know that periods of idleness can result in obesity, but Heinrich makes the case that a prolonged sedentary lifestyle has negative consequences on our bones. If bones don't receive the normal daily stress that comes from moving and running, they will become weak (osteoporosis). Think about astronauts who live in the zero-gravity environment of space for a period. Their bones become weak rapidly. Like pronghorns, we weren't made to be sedentary. We were made to play.

If you raise some rats in a dull, solitary environment and then raise others in a stimulating environment filled with toys, guess what happens? Over time, the rats have been raised and kept in an enriched environment have larger brains than the rats in confinement. This was the result of a landmark paper in 1964 by Marion Diamond and her colleagues. Specifically, they showed that a stimulating environment increased the depth of a rat's cerebral cortex. The article was one of the first to show the benefits of play.

Dr. Stuart Brown, the founder of the National Institute of Play, defines play as "something done for its own sake." Brown goes on to explain, "It's voluntary, it's pleasurable, it offers a sense of engagement, it takes you out of time. And the act itself is more important than the outcome."

Did you hear that last sentence? The act of playing is more important than the outcome.

Adult play helps us maintain our social well-being. Play builds community and connection. If play helps to teach children about cooperation and sharing, it only makes sense that the extension of play into adulthood does the same thing. Besides building friendships, play keeps the mind sharp and can be quite therapeutic. Research shows that adults who play may feel the same stressors as adults who do not play. However, those playful adults react to stressful situations in a much healthier way.

The Outdoor Foundation reported that in the average year, 48.9% of Americans ages six and older participate in outdoor activities. Only 22% of these people get out two or more times a week. By contrast, children between the ages of eight to eighteen years spend more than six hours per day with some sort of electronic media. Many have lost their appreciation of nature because indoor activities and technologies, such as cell phones, video games, computers, and movies, dominate their time and interests. Recreating in and learning about nature can help reverse this trend. Richard Louv states in his book, *Last Child in the Woods: Saving Our Children from Nature-Deficit Disorder*, that we must save an endangered indicator species to save environmentalism. That species is the "child in nature." This "child" is slowly becoming the adult in nature.

The U.S. National Park Service launched a successful campaign in 2016 called #FindYourPark to celebrate the 100th birthday of the park service. The idea was to find a national park to visit and appreciate. We think the better slogan would be #FindTheOutside. Find that place where you can sit and observe. Find that place where you can watch, listen, and smell. Find that place in nature where you can learn. Understanding and learning lead to appreciation, and appreciation leads to conservation. Slow down and take your time.

Acknowledgments

We are deeply grateful to all of the people who have made *Project Yellowstone* a successful enrichment program. First, we are grateful to our wives and families for allowing us to travel each summer. Thank you to Katie for reviewing many grant applications and manuscripts. We are especially thankful to those organizations that have supported this program, including Statesville High School, Iredell-Statesville Schools, Mitchell Community College, Boys and Girls Club of the Piedmont, Statesville Rotary Club, Rotary Club of Statesville Fourth Creek, Iredell County Community Foundation, Johnson Foundation, and Statesville Kiwanis Club. Thanks also to those individuals who have supported and continue to support the scholarship fund so that we can take students. We are fortunate to have had excellent leaders that have traveled with us, including Danny Collins, Chris Bowen, Nelson Cooper, Harry Efird, John Ervin, John Karriker, Tracy Snider, and Earl Spencer. We have met many experts that have generously shared their time with us while in the park. These include Dan Hartman, Rick McIntyre, Nathan Varley, and Beth Taylor. Finally, thanks to all the participants who have joined us in this adventure.

Sources and Further Reading

Chapter 1: Cold Times

Agassiz, L., & Bettannier, J. (1840). *Etudes sur les glaciers.* Jent et Gassmann.

Church, S. A., Kraus, J. M., Mitchell, J. C., Church, D. R., & Taylor, D. R. (2003). Evidence for multiple Pleistocene refugia in the postglacial expansion of the eastern tiger salamander, Ambystoma tigrinum tigrinum. *Evolution,* 57(2), 372-383.

Raven, P. H. (1972). Plant species disjunctions: a summary. *Annals of the Missouri Botanical Garden,* 59(2), 234-246.

Chapter 2: Searching for Shortia

Dobbs, David. (2011). How Charles Darwin Seduced Asa Gray. Wired. Accessed from http://www.wired.com/2011/04/how-charles-darwin-seduced-asa-gray/

Jenkins, Charles F. (1942). Asa Gray and His Quest for Shortia Galactacifolia. Arnoldia, 2:13-28.

Troyer, James R. (2001). The Hyams family, father and sons, contributors to North Carolina botany. *Journ. Elisha Mitchell Sci. Soc.* 117(4): 240-248.

Chapter 3: Something Hotter

Hutton, J. (1795). *Theory of the earth: With proofs and illustrations (Vol. 1).* Library of Alexandria.

Lowenstern, J. B., & Hurwitz, S. (2008). Monitoring a supervolcano in repose: Heat and volatile flux at the Yellowstone Caldera. *Elements,* 4(1), 35-40.

Lowenstern, J. B., Smith, R. B., & Hill, D. P. (2006). Monitoring super-volcanoes: geophysical and geochemical signals at Yellowstone and other large caldera systems. *Philosophical*

Transactions of the Royal Society of London A: Mathematical, Physical and Engineering Sciences, 364(1845), 2055-2072.

Lyell, C. (1837). *Principles of geology: Being an inquiry how far the former changes of the Earth's surface are referable to causes now in operation (Vol. 1)*. J. Kay, jun. & brother.

Chapter 5: Fire Flies

Collins, N. C. (1977). Mechanisms Determining the relative Abundance of Brine Flies (Diptera: Ephydridae) in Yellowstone Thermal Spring Effluents. *The Canadian Entomologist*, 109: 415-422.

Collins, N. C. (1975). Tactics of Host Exploitation by a Thermophilic Water Mite. Miscellaneous Publications, *Canadian Entomological Society*, 9: 250-254.

Chapter 6: Ancient Benefits

Brock, T. D. (1997). The value of basic research: discovery of Thermus aquaticus and other extreme thermophiles. *Genetics*, 146(4), 1207-1210.

Brock, T. D. (1995). The road to Yellowstone—and beyond. *Annual Reviews in Microbiology*, 49(1), 1-29.

Rothschild, L. J., & Mancinelli, R. L. (2001). Life in extreme environments. Nature, 409(6823), 1092-1101.

Chapter 7: If You Give a Moose a Tapeworm

Joly, D. and Messier, F. (2004). The Distribution of Echinococcus granulosis in Moose: Evidence for Parasite-induced Vulnerability to Predation by Wolves. *Population Ecology*, 140: 586-590.

Mech, D. (1970). *The Wolf: The Ecology and Behavior of an Endangered Species*. Natural History Press, New York.

Peterson, R. (1977). Wolf Ecology and Prey Relationships on Isle Royale. National Park Service Monograph no. 11, Washington, D. C.

Chapter 9: Lichen this Relationship

Heckman, D. S. et al. (2001). Molecular Evidence for the Early Colonization of Land by Fungi and Plants. *Science*, 293: 1129-1133.

Reece, J. B. et al. (2014). *Campbell Biology*. Boston: Benjamin Cummings/Pearson.

Chapter 10: Hot Pines, a Fungus, and a Beetle

Barringer, L. E., Tomback, D. F., Wunder, M. B., & McKinney, S. T. (2012). Whitebark Pine Stand Condition, Tree Abundance, and Cone Production as Predictors of Visitation by Clark's Nutcracker. *PLoS ONE*, 7(5), e37663. http://doi.org/10.1371/journal.pone.0037663

Geiszler, D. R. et al. (1980). Fire, Fungi, and Beetle Influences on a Lodgepole Pine Ecosystem of South-Central Oregon. *Oecologia* 46.2: 239–243.

Hamer, D., & Pengelly, I. (2015). Whitebark Pine (Pinus albicaulis) Seeds as Food for Bears (Ursus spp.) in Banff National Park, Alberta. *The Canadian Field Naturalist*, 129, 8–14.

Logan, J. A., Macfarlane, W. W., & Willcox, L. (2010). Whitebark pine vulnerability to climate-driven mountain pine beetle disturbance in the Greater Yellowstone Ecosystem. *Ecological Applications*, 20(4), 895–902. http://doi.org/10.1890/09-0655.1

Lotan, James E. (1976). Cone Serotiny-Fire Relationships in Lodgepole Pine. *Proc. Tall Timbers Fire Ecology Conference* 14: 267–278. Print.

Lotan, James E., James K. Brown, and Leon F. Neuenschwander. (1985) *Role of Fire in Lodgepole Pine Forests*. The Bark Beetles, Fuels, and Fire Bibliography: 134–152. Print.

Chapter 11: More than a Snack

Burton, R., Sarks, K., & Peters, D. (1980). The army cutworm. Agriculture Experiment Station, Division of Agriculture, Oklahoma State University. Bulletin B749.

Kevan, P. G., & Kendall, D. M. (1997). Liquid assets for fat bankers: summer nectarivory by migratory moths in the Rocky Mountains, Colorado, USA. Arctic and Alpine Research, 478-482.

Snow, S. J. (1925). Observations on the cutworm, Euxoa auxiliaris Grote, and its principal parasites. *Journal of Economic Entomology*, 18(4), 602-609.

White Jr, D., Kendall, K. C., & Picton, H. D. (1999). Potential energetic effects of mountain climbers on foraging grizzly bears. *Wildlife Society Bulletin*, 146-151.

Chapter 12: Wolves of the Sky

Kabadayi, C., & Osvath, M. (2017). Ravens parallel great apes in flexible planning for tool-use and bartering. *Science*, 357(6347), 202-204.

Heinrich, B. (1995). An experimental investigation of insight in common ravens (Corvus corax). *The Auk*, 994-1003.

Heinrich, B., & Marzluff, J. M. (1991). Do common ravens yell because they want to attract others? *Behavioral Ecology and Sociobiology*, 28(1), 13-21.

Marzluff, J. M., & Heinrich, B. (1991). Foraging by common ravens in the presence and absence of territory holders: an experimental analysis of social foraging. *Animal Behaviour*, 42(5), 755-770.

Stahler, D., Heinrich, B., & Smith, D. (2002). Common ravens, Corvus corax, preferentially associate with grey wolves, Canis lupus, as a foraging strategy in winter. *Animal Behaviour*, 64(2), 283-290.

Wilmers, C. C., Stahler, D. R., Crabtree, R. L., Smith, D. W., & Getz, W. M. (2003). Resource dispersion and consumer dominance: scavenging at wolf-and hunter-killed carcasses in Greater Yellowstone, USA. *Ecology Letters*, 6(11), 996-1003.

Chapter 13: Diggers and Chasers

Amend, S. R. (1970). On the population ecology of Uinta ground squirrels.

Balph, D. M. (1965). Sound Communication in the Uinta Ground Squirrel.

Balph, D. M., & Balph, D. F. (1966). Sound communication of Uinta ground squirrels. *Journal of Mammalogy*, 47(3), 440-450.

Minta, S. C., Minta, K. A., & Lott, D. F. (1992). Hunting associations between badgers (Taxidea taxus) and coyotes (Canis latrans). *Journal of Mammalogy*, 73(4), 814-820.

Chapter 15: Guilty and Never Proven Innocent

Bartholomew, J. L., & Reno, P. W. (2002). The history and dissemination of whirling disease. In American Fisheries Society Symposium (pp. 3-24). American Fisheries Society.

Chapter 16: Extreme Weapons

Allen, J.A., and J.S. Levinton. (2007). Costs of bearing a sexually selected ornamental weapon in a fiddler crab. *Functional Ecology*, 21: 154–161.

Arnold, S. (1994). Is there a unifying concept of sexual selection that applies to both plants and animals? *The American Naturalist*, 144:1-12.

Baskin, J. (1980). Evolutionary reversal in Mylagaulus (Mammalia, Rodentia) from the late Miocene of Florida. *American Midland Naturalist*, 104:155-162.

Birkhead, T. (2000). *Promiscuity: An Evolutionary History of Sperm Competition.* Cambridge, MA: Harvard University Press.

Cook, H. and Gregory, J. (1941). Mesogaulus praecursor, a new rodent from the Miocene of Nebraska. *Journal of Paleontology,* 15:549-552.

Darwin, C. R. (1859). *On the Origin of Species.* Vol. XI. e Harvard Classics. New York, NY: P. F. Collier and Son, 1909–14.

Emlen, D. (2001). Costs and the diversification of exaggerated animal structures. *Science,* 291:1534-1536.

Emlen, D. (2014). Animal Weapons: The Evolution of Battle. New York, NY: Henry Holt and Company.

Hopkins, S. (2005). The evolution of fossoriality and the adaptive role of horns in the Mylagaulidae (Mammalia: Rodentia). *Proceedings of the Royal B,* 272:1705-1713.

Hyatt, G.W., and M. Salmon. (1978). Combat in the fiddler crabs Uca pugilator and U. pugnax: A quantitative analysis. *Behaviour,* 65: 182–211.

Judson, O. (2002). *Dr. Tatiana's Sex Advice to all Creation.* New York: Henry Holt and Company, LLC.

Korth, W. (1994). *The Tertiary Record of Rodents in North America.* New York: Plenum Press.

Korth, W. (1999). Hesperogaulus, a new genus of Mylagaulid Rodent (Mammalia) from the Miocene (Barstovian to Hemphillian) of the Great Basin. *Journal of Paleontology,* 73:945-951.

Lundrigan, B. (1996). Morphology of horns and fighting behavior in the family Bovidae. *Journal of Mammalogy,* 77:462-475.

Picard, K., Thomas, D., Festa-Bianchet, M., and Lanthier, C. (1994). Bovid horns: An important site for heat loss during winter? *Journal of Mammalogy,* 75:710-713.

Shotwell, J. (1958). Evolution and biogeography of Aplodontid and Mylagaulid rodents. Evolution, 12:451-484.

Chapter 17: Mud Nests

Andersson, M. (1982). Sexual selection, natural selection and quality advertisement. *Biol. J. Linn. Soc.*, 17:375-393.

Brown, C. R., Brown, C. R., Brown, M. B., & Brown, M. B. (2000). Breeding habitat selection in cliff swallows: the effect of conspecific reproductive success on colony choice. *Journal of Animal Ecology*, 133–142.

Brown, C. R., & Brown, M. B. (1992). Ectoparasitism as a cause of natal dispersal in cliff swallows. *Ecology*, 73(5), 1718–1723. http://doi.org/10.2307/1940023

Dawkins, R. (1982). *The Extended Phenotype.* Oxford: Oxford University Press.

Mainwaring, M. C., Hartley, I. R., Lambrechts, M. M., & Deeming, D. C. (2014). The design and function of birds' nests. *Ecology and Evolution*, 4(20), 3909–28.

Chapter 18: Animal Funerals

Anderson, J. R., Gillies, A., & Lock, L. C. (2010). Pan thanatology. *Current Biology*, 20(8), R349-R351.

Biro, D., Humle, T., Koops, K., Sousa, C., Hayashi, M., & Matsuzawa, T. (2010). Chimpanzee mothers at Bossou, Guinea carry the mummified remains of their dead infants. *Current Biology*, 20(8), R351-R352.

Franke, M. A. (2005). *To save the wild bison: Life on the edge in Yellowstone.* University of Oklahoma Press.

Iglesias, T. L., McElreath, R., & Patricelli, G. L. (2012). Western scrub-jay funerals: cacophonous aggregations in response to dead conspecifics. *Animal behaviour*, 84(5), 1103-1111.

Lott, D. F. (2003). American bison: a natural history (Vol. 6). University of California Press.

McComb, K., Baker, L., & Moss, C. (2006). African elephants show high levels of interest in the skulls and ivory of their own species. *Biology Letters*, 2(1), 26-28.

Chapter 19: Outrunning Ghosts

Byers, J. A. (1997). *American Pronghorn: Social Adaptations and the Ghosts of Predators Past*. University of Chicago Press.

Donlan, J. (2005). Re-wilding North America. *Nature*, 436(7053), 913-914.

Donlan, J., C., Berger, J., Bock, C. E., Bock, J. H., Burney, D. A., Estes, J. A., ... & Soulé, M. E. (2006). Pleistocene rewilding: an optimistic agenda for twenty-first century conservation. *The American Naturalist*, 168(5), 660-681.

Gilbert, S. L., Sivy, K. J., Pozzanghera, C. B., DuBour, A., Over-duijn, K., Smith, M. M., ... & Prugh, L. R. (2017). Socioeconomic Benefits of Large Carnivore Recolonization Through Reduced Wildlife-Vehicle Collisions. *Conservation Letters*, 10(4), 431-439.

Janis, C. M., & Fortelius, M. (1988). On the means whereby mammals achieve increased functional durability of their dentitions, with special reference to limiting factors. *Biological Reviews*, 63(2), 197-230.

Stuart, A. J. (1991). Mammalian extinctions in the Late Pleistocene of Northern Eurasia and North America. *Biological Reviews*, 66(4), 453-562.

Webb, S. D. (1977). A history of savanna vertebrates in the New World. Part I: North America. *Annual Review of Ecology and Systematics*, 8(1), 355-380.

Chapter 20: Persistance Pays Off
Chapter 21: Reintroduction Interactions

Bekoff, M. (1977). Canis latrans. *Mammal Species*, 79:1-9.

Bollin-Booth, H. A. 2007. Diet analysis of the coyote (Canis latrans) in metropolitan park systems of northeast Ohio. Master's thesis. Cleveland State University, Ohio.

Crooks, K. R., and M. E. Soule. (1999). Mesopredator release and avifaunal extinctions in a fragmented system. *Nature*, 400: 563-566.

Flores, D. (2016). *Coyote America: A Natural and Supernatural History.* Basic Books: New York, NY.

Gehrt, S. D. (2007). Biology of coyotes in urban landscapes. Pages 303-311 in D. L. Nolte, W.M. Arjo, and D. H. Stalman, eds. Proceedings of the 12th Wildlife Damage Management Conference. Corpus Christi, TX.

Heinrich, R.E., Strait, S.G., and Houde, P. (2008). Earliest Eocene Miacidae (Mammalia: Carnivora) from northwestern Wyoming. *Journal of Paleontology*, 82: 154–162.

Howell, R. G. (1982). The urban coyote problem in Los Angelos County. Pages 21-23 in R. E. Marsh, ed. Proceedings of the tenth Vertebrate Pest Conference. University of California, Davis.

Kays, R. et al. (2015). Cats are rare where coyotes roam. *Journal of Mammalogy*, 96: 981-987.

Kays, R., Curtis, A., and Kirchman, J. (2010). Rapid adaptive evolution of northeastern coyotes via hybridization with wolves. *Biology Letters*, 6:89-93.

Kilgo, J., Ray, S., Vukovich, M., Goode, M., and Ruth, C. (2012). *Wildlife Management*, 76:1420-1430.

Knowlton, F. F., E. M. Gese, and M. M. Jaeger. (1999). Coyote depradation control: An interface between biology and management. *Journal of Range Management*, 52: 398-412.

MacCracken, J. G. (1982). Coyote foods in a Southern California suburb. *Wildlife Society Bulletin*, 10: 280-281.

McClure, M. F. et al. (1995). Diets of coyotes near the boundary of Saguaro national monument and Tucson, Arizona. *Southwestern Naturalist*, 40: 101-104.

Meachen, J. and Samuels, J. (2012). Evolution in coyotes (Canis latrans) megafaunal extinctions. *PNAS*, 109: 4194-4196.

Meachen, J., Janowicz, A., Avery, J., and Sandleir, R. (2014). Ecological Changes in Coyotes (Canis latrans) in Response to the Ice Age Megafaunal Extinctions. *PLoS ONE*,9(12): e116041. doi:10. 1371/journal.pone.0116041

Mech, L. D. (1974). Canis lupus. *Mammal Species*, 37:1-6.

Merkle, J. A., Stahler, D. R., and Smith, D. W. (2009). Interference Competition Between Gray Wolves and Coyotes in Yellowstone National Park. *Canadian Journal of Zoology*, 87: 56-63.

VonHoldt, B. M. et al. (2011). A Genome-Wide Perspective on the Evolutionary History of Enigmatic Wolf-Like Canids. *Genome Research*, 8: 1294-1305.

Wang, X. et al. (2010). Aggression and Rabid Coyotes, Massachusetts, USA. *Emerging Infectious Diseases*, 16: 357-369.

White, L. A., & Gehrt, S. D. (2009). Coyote Attacks on Humans in the United States and Canada. *Human Dimensions of Wildlife*, 14(6), 419–432. http://doi.org/10.1080/10871200903055326

Suggested Readings

Gehrt, S. D., Wilson, E. C., Brown, J. L., & Anchor, C. (2013). Population Ecology of Free-Roaming Cats and Interference Competition by Coyotes in Urban Parks. *PLoS ONE*, 8(9), e75718–11.

Gehrt, S. D., C. Anchor, and L. A. White. (2009). Home range and landscape use of coyotes in a major metropolitan landscape: Coexistence or conflict? *Journal of Mammalogy*, 90: 1045-1057.

Gehrt, S. D., & Prange, S. (2006). Interference competition between coyotes and raccoons: a test of the mesopredator release hypothesis. *Behavioral Ecology*, 18(1), 204–214.

Heinrich, R.E., Strait, S.G., and Houde, P. (2008). Earliest Eocene Miacidae (Mammalia: Carnivora) from northwestern Wyoming. *Journal of Paleontology*, 82: 154–162.

Kays, R., Curtis, A., and Kirchman, J. (2010). Rapid adaptive evolution of northeastern coyotes via hybridization with wolves. *Biology Letters*, 6:89-93.

Kilgo, J., Ray, S., Vukovich, M., Goode, M., and Ruth, C. (2012). *Wildlife Management*, 76:1420-1430.

Meachen, J., Janowicz, A., Avery, J., and Sandleir, R. (2014). Ecological Changes in Coyotes (Canis latrans) in Response to the Ice Age Megafaunal Extinctions. *PLoS ONE*, 9(12): e116041.

Meachen, J. and Samuels, J. (2012). Evolution in coyotes (Canis latrans) megafaunal extinctions. *PNAS*, 109: 4194-4196.

Newsome, S. D., Garbe, H. M., Wilson, E. C., & Gehrt, S. D. (2015). Individual variation in anthropogenic resource use in an urban carnivore. *Oecologia*, 178(1), 115–128.

Tallian, A., Smith, D. W., Stahler, D. R., Metz, M. C., Wallen, R. L., Geremia, C., et al. (2017). Predator foraging response to a resurgent dangerous prey. *Functional Ecology*, 96, 1151–12.

Chapter 25: Playing in Wild Places

Byers, J. A. (1997). *American Pronghorn: Social Adaptations and the Ghosts of Predators Past*. University of Chicago Press.

Diamond, M. C., Krech, D., & Rosenzweig, M. R. (1964). The effects of an enriched environment on the histology of the rat cerebral cortex. *Journal of Comparative Neurology*, 123(1), 111-119.

Louv, R. (2008). *Last Child in the Woods: Saving Our Children from Nature-Deficit Disorder.* Chapel Hill, NC: Algonquin Books. 390 pp.

Magnuson, C. D., & Barnett, L. A. (2013). The playful advantage: How playfulness enhances coping with stress. *Leisure Sciences,* 35(2), 129-144.

Roberts, D., U. Foehr, and V. Rideout. (2005) Generation M: Media in the Lives of 8 to 18 year Olds. Kaiser Family Foundation. 145 pp. The report is available online at: http://www.kff.org/entmedia/upload/generation-m-media-in-the-lives-of-8-18-year-olds-report.pdf

The Outdoor Foundation. (2010). Outdoor Recreation Participation Report 2010. The Outdoor Foundation. 68 pp. The report is available online at: http://www.outdoorfoundation.org/pdf/ResearchParticipation2010.pdf.

Figures

3.1. Yellowstone caldera

By Kbh3rd [Public domain], via Wikimedia Commons

4.1. Eukaryotic cell

By OpenStax [CC BY 4.0 (http://creativecommons.org/licenses/by/4.0)], via Wikimedia Commons

4.2. Prokaryotic cell

By CNX OpenStax [CC BY 4.0], via Wikimedia Commons

5.1. Mite life cycle

Mite Life Cycle by Bugboy52.4 (Own work) [GFDL (http://www.gnu.org/copyleft/fdl.html) or CC BY-SA 4.0-3.0-2.5-2.0-1.0, via Wikimedia Commons

6.1. Gel electrophoresis

By Jennifer0328 (Own work) [CC BY-SA 4.0], via Wikimedia Commons

7.1. *E. granulosis*

By CDC/Dr. L.L.A. Moore, Jr [Public domain], via Wikimedia Commons

8.3. Endosymbiotic theory

By CNX OpenStax [CC BY 4.0 (http://creativecommons.org/licenses/by/4.0)], via Wikimedia Commons

17.1. Mud nests

Photo by Tom Johnson. Used with permission.

22-24. Maps

By U.S. National Park Service, restoration/cleanup by Matt Holly [Public domain], via Wikimedia Commons

Review Questions

Unfinished Business

Chapter 1

1. Why are the southern Appalachian Mountains much more diverse than the northern section? What does this have to do with glaciation?

Chapter 2

1. Explain how the North American-east Asian plant connection supported Darwin's theory of evolution.

Chapter 3

1. Yellowstone's thermal features all have water in common, although some have more than others. Where does this seemingly endless supply of water come from?

2. Fumaroles, or steam vents, are found near the Mud Volcano region of the park. Why would these thermal features be found here?

Chapters 4 and 5

1. List some differences between eukaryotic and prokaryotic cells.

2. How do photosynthetic organisms differ from chemosynthetic organisms?

3. *Partnuniella*, a parasitic mite, has a 10% survival rate in its larval form because of the environment it lives in. With this survival rate, how does it survive from generation to generation?

Chapter 6

1. What are some ways DNA analyses can be used?

Chapter 7

1. Formulate an argument to support the idea that parasites control ecosystems.

Chapter 8

1. How do mitochondria and chloroplasts differ in function?

Chapter 9

1. Explain how lichen relationships could be related to global ice ages.

Chapter 10

1. Why are fires needed for some ecosystems?

Chapter 11

1. If hundreds of thousands of moths migrate to higher elevations every year, why don't all grizzly bears take advantage of this feast?

Chapter 12

1. Why would ravens always be around wolves, but rarely ever around coyotes?

Chapter 13

1. What kind of situations would favor a badger and coyote 'needing' to hunt together?

Chapter 15

1. How would you define an invasive species?

2. Would there be anything wrong with introducing a non-native (or invasive) species to get rid of another invasive species?

3. If a non-native species in an area seems to not cause any ecological problems, should it still be defined as invasive?

4. Kudzu has been here in the U.S. since 1876. How do ecologists define a native species? When does a non-native (even if it is invasive) species become a native species? What do we do with native species that are also invasive?

Chapter 16

1. Charles Darwin wrote the following in the *Origin of Species* in 1859:

> How low in the scale of nature this law of battle descends, I know not; male alligators have been described as fighting, bellowing, and whirling round, like Indians in a war-dance, for the possession of the females; male salmons have been seen fighting all day long; male stag-beetles often bear wounds from the huge mandibles of other males. The war is, perhaps, severest between the males of polygamous animals, and these seem oftenest provided with special weapons.

Explain why the last sentence would make sense.

2. List as many specific animals you can think of that have elaborate structures that could be used as weapons. Also, describe whether these structures are found in both males and females or just one sex.

3. Male moose allocate important minerals like phosphorus and calcium to growing antlers. Engaging in a fight could leave a bull

moose vulnerable? Would it be possible for elaborate structures to be used mostly to deter, or warn, rival males?

4. Scientists often work hard to understand the connection between structure and function to fitness/evolutionary potential. When it comes to the bull moose or bighorn rams, explain how structure complements function and also how structure limits function.

5. Doug Emlen, in his book *Animal Weapons*, states the following:

> As weapons get bigger they select for increasingly elaborate deterrence, and deterrence, in turn, selects for bigger and bigger weapons. Arms races and deterrence push each other forward, escalating in an evolutionary spiral.

Please explain this statement.

Chapter 17

1. Observe one cliff swallow nest for 3 minutes. How many times does the swallow enter and leave within that time period?

Chapter 18

1. Do you think it is possible for animals to express emotions? Why or why not?

Chapter 19

1. What do you think about rewilding the American west? Are there legitimate reasons to follow through with introducing some of these larger animals?

2. Why are American pronghorn much faster than their predators?

Chapter 20

1. List several ways coyotes have thrived even though they have been heavily persecuted.

2. When it comes to feeding, coyotes are referred to as "ecological generalists." Explain what this means.

Chapter 21

1. What was the rationale behind introducing wolves to the Greater Yellowstone Ecosystem?

2. Explain what a keystone species is and why they are essential to their particular ecosystem.

3. Acclimation pens were used for wolves during the reintroduction process. Please explain why these were used.

4. Wolf #8 showed a rare type of social behavior by adopting o spring that were not his own. Why would this behavior be rare in mammals? How could this be a beneficial behavior?

5. Wolf #21 was obviously very successful at reproducing. Come up with a couple hypotheses as to what made him this successful. How do you think he was able to hold his alpha status for so long?

6. Wolf #21's pack of 37 wolves did not last. Knowing what you know about factors that limit population growth, why was this so? What is the difference between interspecific and intraspecific competition?

About the Authors

Parks Collins and Bill Day lead summer expeditions to Yellowstone for a small community college. They are both nature lovers and Yellowstone addicts.

Parks started *Project Yellowstone* in 2009. He is a fan of large trees and intelligent birds. When not in Yellowstone or reading about Yellowstone, he can be found teaching in a classroom or hanging cameras in the woods. Parks and his wife, Katie, are trying to raise three kids that aren't afraid of coyotes.

Bill, nature and wildlife enthusiast, is a leader and developer with *Project Yellowstone*. He designs hikes and leads discussions related to the ecology and geology of the park. He is a trained wildlife spotter. During his day job, he assesses road conditions. Several times each week, he entertains millions worldwide by talking into a microphone. Bill and his wife, Danielle, also have three kids.